# Talking Trash:
## My Year In Zero-Wasteland

JAREN CERF

ISBN: 978-1-9995624-1-0

Consulting Editor: Martin Melhuish
Editor: One Love Editing
Cover Art: Maria Hidalgo Casamayor

# DEDICATION

For Lilu and Arlo. I will do whatever it takes to make this world a better place for you.

And for Marty. Thank you for believing I was a writer the entire time.

# CONTENTS

JAREN CERF

# ACKNOWLEDGMENTS

Special thanks to Martin Melhuish for never doubting I would finish this book, and for your time and belief in this project. I can't believe it's finally here!

Thanks to Bea Johnson, the author of *Zero Waste Home*, and Kirsten Dirksen of www.faircompanies.com, for inspiring me to look at the world differently.

Thanks to Marie Rayma, the author of *Make It Up*, for introducing me to natural beauty and soapmaking!

Thanks to my editor, Sandra, for your encouragement.

To Maria, your talent as a graphic designer never ceases to amaze me.

Thanks to my friends and family for letting me talk their ears off about zero-waste living for the last few years. I can't believe no one ever told me to zip it, already.

And finally, thank *you* for opening the pages of this book and joining me on this crazy journey.

# FOREWORD
## BY MARTIN MELHUISH

"What would Jaren do?"

Have to admit, it's a question I have asked myself a few times when making purchasing decisions based on the packaging involved (i.e. potential waste) since reading the manuscript for Talking Trash: My Year in Zero-Wasteland for the first time. Jaren Cerf is an inspirational character to begin with, but on the topic of personal waste management, she'll also tweak your social conscience.

"You get this overwhelming guilt and you begin thinking about your own lifestyle and you start getting thoroughly depressed," says Jaren, who is also a successful, much-traveled singer, musician, songwriter, and creative entrepreneur. "But then you start thinking, 'Well, if I can do this and I can do that, and if I only do 30 percent of what is suggested, that will make a lot of difference over time.' Multiply that by the number of people who take a similar view and you now have a massive change in wind direction. That's why I want everything to be solution-based because, even if you are super busy, you can still make some impactful changes with minimum disruption to your daily routine."

The appeal of Jaren's informative, entertaining, and often amusing journal is that it is written from personal experience arising from a general do-it-yourself attitude which has been part of her DNA since she was a youngster growing up in Laramie, Wyoming. The west was built, for the most part, on the self-reliance and resourcefulness of its earliest settlers, and before you get too far along in this book, you are going to recognize those traits in Jaren's propensity for DIY in most areas of her life.

But, as she is quick to point out, she is not 100 percent zero waste, and neither is she trying to preach perfection. She describes herself as simply a mom who is trying her best every day to make a difference. "I think in society, it is too easy to feel like shit if you fall off the train," she once told me during a chat on this subject. "I want to tell people, 'Don't feel bad if you fall off! Get back on, one thing at a time!' We don't have to be perfect about it."

Though there have been various environmental movements that warned of the dangers of waste pollution to our fragile planet dating back to before the turn of the last century, the consumerism that accompanied the post-war economic boom in America contained the seeds of discontent expressed by a growing number of skeptics who saw a negative and destructive side of things in all that prosperity.

"A society in which consumption has to be artificially stimulated in order to keep production going is a society founded on trash and waste, and such a society is a house built on sand," suggested author and playwright Dorothy L. Sayers in her 1947 book, Creed or Chaos.

Best-selling author and social critic Vance Packard espoused a similar viewpoint in his book The Waste Makers, which predicted the rise of the American consumer culture. It was published almost six decades ago in 1960, yet his narrative at the time about the concept of planned obsolescence and "the systematic attempt of business to make us wasteful, debt-ridden, permanently discontented individuals" still ring true in a political climate where, in the name of corporate profits, regulatory laws are being rolled back and the environment, rather than being protected, is being left to fend for itself.

Even more frightening was Packard's statement that "the uncomfortably challenging point to be recognized [is] that perhaps the United States has no acceptable alternative to ever-rising and wasteful consumption." He cited a viewpoint expressed by "dispassionate social observer" John Kouwenhoven in a Harper's article entitled, "Waste Not, Have Not – A Clue to American Prosperity," that "we may not be able to get rid of the mess without also getting rid of abundance."

According to Packard's research at the time, the average American family was throwing away about 750 metal cans each year, and each individual man, woman, and child was using up to an average of eighteen tons of materials a year. "In the Orient," he pointed out, "a family lucky enough to gain possession of a metal can treasures it and puts it to work in some way, if only as a flower pot."

On Christmas Eve 1968, during NASA's Apollo 8 mission which was the first to go "Round the moon and back," crew member William A. Anders took a photograph, dubbed "Earthrise," which many have credited with giving renewed impetus to the environmental movement. It was a picture of planet earth, blue, finite, and fragile, but oh so welcoming, rising out of the blackness of space over the desolate and forbidding surface of the moon in the foreground.

In Life magazine's 100 Photographs That Changed the World book, nature photographer Galen Rowell called it, "the most influential environmental photograph ever taken." It was the first time that an image of earth had been captured from that perspective, and it was compelling in its revelation of how small and delicate our planet really is. It changed the perception that earth has an infinite capacity to absorb the detritus and dreck produced daily by humanity.

Looking back at the 70s, especially the early years of the decade, the music world was inspired to make comment by this renewed focus on the environment and the fragility of the planet. In February of 1979, Canadian radio personality Doug Pringle and I spent time with Marvin Gaye in Los Angeles. It was eight years after he'd released the track "Mercy Mercy Me (The Ecology)" on his masterpiece of an album What's Going On. The early 70s had been a transitional time in his life. Berry Gordy Jr., the head of his record label Motown, hated the record, but Marvin said that he'd had a spiritual awakening and he was not going to be coerced into going back—at that point anyway—into writing songs about his "erotic fantasies" given the chaos he saw in the world at the time.

Other songs of the early 70s addressing environmental issues included "Nature's Way," Spirit (following their 1968 song "Fresh Garbage"); "Big Yellow Taxi," Joni Mitchell; "Ecology Song," Stephen Stills; "Lady Run Lady Hide," April Wine; "Before the Deluge," Jackson Browne; "Never Turn Your Back On Mother Earth," Sparks, and, in the late 70s, the epic "Nuclear Apathy," Crack the Sky. For a while, the ecology was getting some front-window exposure as part of the pop culture.

Population Bomb, the controversial but impactful book by Stanford University Professor Paul Ehrlich and his wife, Anne (uncredited), published in 1968, had warned about overpopulation and the environmental damage that would inevitably result from a population too large for Earth to support. There are an estimated 7.5 billion people inhabiting our planet today. It's a number that is expected to rise to 11.2 billion by the year 2100. With stats like that, it doesn't take a clairvoyant to see that waste management will have to be a priority for governments of the world in the future as well as a necessary lifestyle consideration for individuals who care about the quality of life today and for future generations.

A few years ago, one of those concerned individuals, Australian sailor Ivan MacFadyen, told of his horror during a yacht race between Melbourne and Osaka at the "severe lack of marine life and copious amounts of rubbish" he encountered. Speaking to Guardian Australia, MacFadyen described looking down and seeing all manner of garbage shimmering in the depths below, up to 20 meters under the water. "We went on to the U.S. and back again. We did 23,000 miles [37,000 kms] and I'd say 7,000 of those were in garbage. The boat is still damaged from it. We had to free the rudder of rubbish one night, which was scary. We were terrified of something ripping a hole in the boat."

He concluded: "Humans are such a blight on the planet that we will just trash an area because it is out of sight most of the time. It completely changed the way I look at things. I used to chuck rubbish away without thinking twice, but there's no way I will do that now."

For author and environmental activist Jaren Cerf, who is also the mother of two young children, this issue is also a real and present concern that is never far from her mind.

\*\*\*\*\*\*

I first met Jaren Cerf in the summer of 2015 when she auditioned for a theatrical musical I had written titled OH CANADA What A Feeling! – A Musical Odyssey. She ultimately joined the cast and earned rave reviews for her vocal range, charismatic presence, and versatility in portraying Joni Mitchell—actually one of the songs she sang was the aforementioned "Big Yellow Taxi"—and Celine Dion in the show, which opened at Caesars Windsor prior to a critically acclaimed two-week run at the Princess of Wales Theatre in Toronto.

We became friends during the course of the show and stayed in touch afterwards, frequently spending time chatting about music and the arts, often brainstorming on creative ideas and concepts that we could work on together. And as the earliest of those chats played out, I began to understand that the woman who I had simply considered an extraordinarily talented singer struggling to find her niche in the music world had been there, done that, and got the T-shirt, which was no doubt eco-friendly and recycled. Yes, I was also discovering her passion for environmental issues.

Jaren, in fact, had already lived the life of an international pop star, and the more than fifty million views of her music videos on YouTube, thousands of followers worldwide on social media, and numerous award nominations and top-of-the-chart Billboard hits in the EDM/Trance world, in which she continues to be revered, attest to that.

She first mentioned a zero-waste project to me just after Christmas 2015, and then, with an idea already formulated in her mind, she sent me this note on January 9, 2016:

> *Hey Marty - I'm trying something out that doesn't take up much time and, by the end of the year, I could have a pretty great book about it. I think I wanna try to become zero waste by the end of the year and see if someone like me could maintain it.*
>
> *I just hammered out a few ideas tonight about the experience so far, and I wondered (if you have five minutes) if you think it could be something.*

I read the chapter that she had "hammered out" in two hours that evening. Did I think it could be something? Does a bear leave deposits of organic, compostable scat in the woods?

In early March 2016, by popular demand, she was back on the road and performing at Trance Vision: Awakening in Moscow, one of the many cities globally she had played previously during a period in her career when she actually required bodyguards at a number of her club performances. Moscow was one of the "zero waste" trips she took during the time of writing the book you hold in your hands. The outfit she wore on stage that night, in keeping with that initiative, was a creation from the House of Jaren... her own DIY design. One of my favorite pictures from that trip is of Jaren sitting in the Geneva airport on a stopover dutifully putting time in on the manuscript, even though the demands of travel and the swirl of emotion around an important live appearance in a foreign country usually preclude extracurricular activities like book writing.

Jaren's artistic versatility is a major part of the story connected to the life and times of this multitalented Canadian/American performer and creative entrepreneur whose credits don't easily fit on a business card: singer, songwriter, musician, recording artist, actress, women's advocate, environmental activist, author, dancer, filmmaker, vocal coach, UX designer and, a little out of left field, championship yodeler. Though not something she kept up, she was also a pretty decent painter in her preteens. Today, if you ask for a thumbnail sketch of her professional competencies and experience, she will tell you that she is simply a storyteller.

Jaren arrived in Canada in 2011 after spending ten years in Los Angeles, following her move from her hometown of Laramie, Wyoming, working in the film and music industry. For a time in LA, she was personal assistant to Golden Globe Award–winning actor Scott Bakula (*Quantum Leap, Star Trek: Enterprise*) and his wife, actress/dancer Chelsea Field (*Masters of the Universe*).

She had continued to pursue her music career, often playing her own original music in lounges with a fake ID because she was underage. In 2005, she met Montreal-based producer/DJ Matt Cerf at a party in LA. It was the turning point in her career as she discovered Trance music and was soon propelled to international fame in that genre with a distinctive voice that one pundit characterized as "haunted by angels and demons alike." The two have, to date, produced close to 125 songs together. Her American toplines (vocal tune and lyrics) paired almost seamlessly with European dance beats, and success in that genre wasn't long in coming.

Renowned Dutch Trance music producer/DJ Armin van Buuren, who has called her "easily one of the best singer/songwriters," picked up one of the songs ("Unforgivable"), which became a worldwide dance hit, effectively launching her career in 2008 as she began to tour with van Buuren, and then on her own in 2009, subsequently earning a number of International Dance Music Awards (IDMA) nominations with trance partners Matt Cerf and Shawn Mitiska. The song "Man On the Run" (Dash Berlin with Cerf, Mitiska & Jaren) from this period has become one of the standards of the Trance music genre.

She had the first of her two children in 2010 and moved to her husband's hometown of Montreal the following year. It was here that she met Sébastian Lefebvre, guitarist/vocalist with the internationally renowned "pop-punk" band Simple Plan, with whom she began writing pop music for a long list of established artists and album projects while still creating material for the dance crowd. In 2013, one of those dance songs, "This Is My Goodbye," performed under her alias Fenja, was number two for three consecutive weeks on the Billboard Dance Club Songs chart for eminent French producer/DJ Antoine Clamaran. In 2014, Jaren cowrote Andee's "We Are Gold," which debuted during the CBC broadcast of the Sochi Olympic Winter Games in February of that year.

In 2015, she completed the recording of her sophomore "folk" album 7 Year Itch, produced in her hometown of Montreal by Sébastien Lefebvre and Swedish musician/composer Rickard Nilsson. It was the follow-up to her 2008 debut recording Fixin' It Upright, which had been recorded in Sweden under the auspices of two of that country's finest producers, Alar Suurna (Roxette) and Jerker Eklund (Jill Johnson).

In late spring 2016, Jaren earned a feature role in the film, Song of Granite, an Irish/Canadian coproduction shot in Ireland and Montreal, which documents the life and times of the late Irish traditional singer Joe Heaney. In March 2017, she performed for TeleFilm Canada in Austin, Texas, at the SXSW (South By Southwest) premiere of the film, and it was here, just by happenstance, that a motivational figure from her past suddenly appeared. While Jaren was having her official picture taken for Getty Images with the cast and crew, next up for his portrait was the star of the popular kids-friendly PBS series from the '90s, Bill Nye the Science Guy, and the crew behind the documentary film Bill Nye: Science Guy, which also had its world premiere at SXSW.

Because of the schedule, she didn't have the opportunity to speak to him, but this was a big moment for Jaren, who, in her youth, had taken some inspiration for her environmentally active, zero-waste ways from the kids' science show Beakman's World (Paul Zaloom) and from Bill Nye himself, who emerged from his series as a tireless advocate for the scientific community and its persistent warnings of the disastrous impact of climate change on the planet. She recalls that about a decade ago, she took great interest in a contest that Bill and his neighbor, actor Ed Begly Jr., were having to see who could maintain the smallest carbon footprint.

"As an adult, I've fallen in love with statistics and studies—probably because my mom recited studies all the time as I was growing up, and my dad is very much into geology and archaeology these days... and I love documentaries. So, when I ran into Bill Nye in Austin, I was over-the-moon excited. I couldn't believe I was seeing him in person. I actually physically pointed him out to my

Irish friends and jumped up and down a few times like a ten-year-old. I have no doubt they remember the incident. But to me, scientists and science communicators like Bill Nye, Neil deGrasse Tyson, David Suzuki and Paul Zaloom (Beakman's World), are our real stars and we need them in our world, front and center."

**Martin Melhuish**
Writer/Author/Creative
Entrepreneur Toronto, Canada
August 2017

Martin Melhuish, who acted as consulting editor on Talking Trash, is the author of more than a dozen books dealing with music and popular culture. In conjunction with companies like Nashville/Toronto-based TH Entertainment, he has also written, directed, and produced documentaries for broadcast networks around the world.

# INTRODUCTION:
## DOWN IN THE DUMPS

*These damned millennials with their organic, free-range this; locally-sourced that; eco-friendly those... You know there's no such thing as zero waste, right? The only thing you can control is how much garbage ends up in your house. What's the point? And anyway, when Yellowstone volcano blows, who's going to care? We'll all be dead. Life's too short and I'm too busy, too broke, and too concerned with more pressing personal matters to give a damn about "global warming." Yeah, like that's a thing. Talk to geologists about the history of ice ages and global events. They've happened before. I'm not sure why you're wasting your time, but good luck, nut job.*

Now, no one has actually uttered those words to me verbatim yet, but I feel like it's only a matter of time. And I could try to craft up a clever reply, sure. But if there's one thing I've learned in my thirty-four years, it's this: You can lead a horse to water, but you can't make it drink. Period.

So what on earth would compel me to take interest in such an extreme way of living?

There are two answers to this question. The first is that if you ask millennials for their thoughts on global warming, the majority of them will tell you we need to take actions to halt it. There isn't a mother my age out there that doesn't want to leave the world a better place for her child. Most of us are scared.

The second reason is that I separated from my husband and am in need of a "project" for when my kids are at his house. You know, to kill time in a healthy way—instead of sobbing uncontrollably while scrolling Facebook pictures of friends who are rocking successful marriages. BUNCHA LIARS! IT'S ALL GOING TO COME CRASHING DOWN! Baaaaaahhhhh!

I'm calm now.

Truly, my fascination with the zero-waste movement began several years ago, thanks to a YouTube video that popped up about Bea Johnson, the author of Zero Waste Home. The video recounted how Bea shopped for groceries using only cloth bags and glass jars. Then it followed as she gave a tour of her beautiful California home. She graciously showed off her living room, her sons' room, her closet, which contained her and her husband's micro-wardrobes—but it was while she gave a tour of her kitchen that my heart stopped.

It was so beautiful.

So simple.

So organized!

My brain was having trouble processing how little clutter there was. Zero-waste living was the answer to my prayers for a clean home and a lifestyle that looked "put together"!

Actually, no! Scratch that.

My fascination with garbage goes way back. Like more than two decades, now that I think about it.

It all started at the dump.

My experience with the dump is different than most people's. I spent a lot of time there as a kid, thanks to my father's interest in restoring historic properties.

Both my parents came from hardworking, homesteading stock. My dad grew up the youngest of three children, raised on a ranch where the attitude was "if it couldn't be fixed with wire, it wasn't worth fixin'." My mother was the only girl in a family of four children. She just wanted to go hunting and fishing like her brothers, so she spent a lot of time outdoors, learning about the environment and tracking bighorn sheep.

The point is, they were resourceful. They were people of the earth. And they wanted to pass that on to their children.

When they divorced after eleven years of marriage, my parents were forced to do a lot of free activities with us while they got back on their feet. This included a lot of biking, playing games like "Guess that Spice," learning sign language—though I'm guessing now that's how my mom tricked us into getting some silence in the house—learning how to repair broken radios and telephones, and just being really present. My dad even dabbled in arts and crafts when I told him that my friend's dad got over his divorce by making a piñata—I wonder if he figured out I made that up. (I'm sure we were big upcyclers before, but this is my first clear memory of transforming something as blah as an oatmeal container into something as cool as a candy cane piñata.)

Oh, the possibilities…

You couldn't argue that we were deprived as kids because we didn't have video games like our friends. We developed life skills before most of our peers. Bragging rights, in my case.

"What age did I learn to drive? Seven. Stick shift. I win."

Where does the dump come in?

As I mentioned earlier, my dad made his money buying run-down old properties and restoring them, often intent on maintaining any remaining historic charm. We lived in these properties while he made the repairs.

The first weeks after a new purchase were always the best, because that's when we'd visit the local dump most often. My dad would load the trailer with whatever he couldn't salvage—or fix with wire and good ol' duct tape—then call us to announce an adventure was in order.

Typically, a trip to the dump would play out something like this:

Dad: *Girls, I loaded up the trailer. We're going to the dump!*

Me and my sister: *Yesssss! What do you think we'll find today?*

Dad: *I'm looking for a lawn mower.*

The drive to the dump would be long and magical as my sister and I daydreamed about what we'd find. We rarely returned empty-handed. We'd pull into the dump and wait to be directed to a numbered pile area by the person in charge. Once we had our directions, the adventure began!

Dad: *Okay, I'll unload the trailer. You girls have fun. Don't let the guards see you. And let me know if you find a lawnmower, will you?*

With that, my sister and I would take off in search of hidden treasures that didn't involve too much digging or require climbing too far up the pile where it stunk the most. We'd steer clear of seagulls and broken glass, anything that might require us getting a tetanus shot later if mom found out, and we always made sure to look under cardboard boxes. That's where we'd go on to find everything from a two-thousand-dollar racing bike and cassette courses on investment banking, to... you guessed it, numerous working lawnmowers.

We'd time our exits when the booth person was busy directing new dump-goers to their piles and couldn't catch us. Then, on the drive home, we'd question why people were so willing to throw away things that could so easily be repaired. What a waste, we thought. Then we'd rejoice about how much money we saved not buying something we weren't going to buy anyway. Except the lawnmower. You always need one of those where I'm from.

So you see, I was being groomed for this zero-waste experiment my entire life, I just didn't know it!

Only now, as I write this, do I realize to what extent my childhood experience of rescuing and repairing one man's trash effected my life. How fortunate I was to see, firsthand, the effects of garbage on the environment. Sure, I liked scavenging, but that's just because people were throwing away stuff that was so easily repairable! It was shocking! And sure, since the 1990s, we've implemented recycling programs, but there was still a dark side.

There were no flowers at the dump.

There were no beautiful smells, or calming sounds.

There were yapping seagulls, rotting carcasses, and smells so foul you were sure you'd collapse from poisoning if you took one more breath.

The dump was where things went to die.

Back to reality. It's December 2015, and I've decided I simply must go on this zero-waste journey.

But how? I have to be realistic here. I'm a single working mother of two toddlers. I don't have a lot of spare time.

I guess the easiest way to do this would be to change one habit per month. That seems fairly failproof. Right?

# CHAPTER ONE:
## BYOPACKAGING
### JANUARY 1, 2016

I've always been a little hippie at heart. I think it's a combination of my years growing up in the Midwest, the daughter of very practical and hardworking parents, and my years living in Los Angeles among all those unrealistically fit, eco-conscious beach bodies. It just sorta seeped into my skin and bones.

I think my first real green action was shopping with reusable grocery bags ten years ago. It was considered cool at the time, and if there was one thing I strived to be, cool was it. I was deep in the music scene and I had an image to uphold, as did all actors and singers living the Hollywood dream, so in order to up the chances of running into actual celebrities—or accidentally being photographed with one in the parking lot—we shopped at Whole Foods and Trader Joe's. Well, Whole Foods when it was pay day, and Trader Joe's when it wasn't. The more reusable shopping bags you carried, the better.

So, I've decided to start my year-long, zero-waste journey where I left off. Sort of. You see, shopping with my own bags is just a little too easy. Anyone can do that. No, I need a real challenge. Something that would make a vegan, keto CrossFitter take notice and give me a little wink of approval.

**I will start shopping with my own containers.**

17

Seems obvious, right? All groceries, clothing, personal care products, you name it, will have to be purchased and stored using my own supply of glass jars or tins, or whatever I have at home. No plastic wrapping like clamshells, no non-recyclable packaging, and absolutely nothing non-compostable. I mean, I'm not an expert here, but this seems to be a good starting point.

I guess I could buy stuff in recyclable plastic, but the recycling system here just isn't as reliable as they say. I've heard figures as high as two-thirds of all the items we put in the recycling bin get thrown away. That's a hard pill to swallow, so I guess I'll have to investigate to see if that's true. In the meantime, the less a product is packaged, the better. That also means I'll have to start saying no to people who want to give me stuff in plastic bags. That's the real challenge.

One of the nice things about living in a fairly big city is that I have access to stores like a little one on St. Laurent Street here in Montreal called Frenco's. It's been around forever, but I only discovered the place last year since I'm an immigrant. It sells most of its inventory, food, and personal care products in bulk. They do provide containers if you need them, but they encourage you to bring your own. Note taken.

Last year, on my first zero-waste attempt—which lasted all of three days—I got all gung ho, purchased enough glass storage containers to weigh down a mule, and very enthusiastically kicked open Frenco's front door for what would be my first and last trip there for a period of nine months.

What I *thought* would happen was that people in the store would ignore me since we were all zero-waste wannabes, right? They might casually glance over to see my hefty collection of glass jars—I was trying to get away from plastics at the time—and think to themselves, *oh look, another normal person like me.* Instead, the door closed rather abruptly, hitting the bag full of jars I was already struggling to carry, causing an almost deafening amount of noise as they nearly broke clanging against each other.

Then it got really quiet. Like, really quiet.

And like a bunch of grazing gazelles, they calmly stopped what they were doing and took a good long look at me.

I tried to act like I knew what I was doing because I don't like talking to people in public and I especially don't like asking for help. (Ask anyone at the Home Depot near my house. I'll walk all fifty aisles in search of wood screws in lieu of actually having to talk to anyone wearing that dumb orange vest. I've always been sensitive to colors.) I filled my jars, making the load even heavier, and only at checkout did I learn I would actually pay a fair amount more since I neglected to have my glassware tared before filling.

*Duck fat! (My alternative to cursing. I'm trying it out.)*

The good thing about buying from bulk stores, however, is that their prices are typically quite a bit less compared to conventional markets. So I'm guessing I didn't get ripped off that bad; it was probably like shopping at Whole Foods.

Hmm.

Months later after searching YouTube videos by other zero wasters, I finally learned the trick to shopping bulk grocers. Are you ready for it? *Cloth drawstring bags. Not glass.* The advantage? Cloth weighs next to nothing and takes up zero space because, *oh yeah,* it can be folded up. It's also washable and won't cut you.

The best part? I'm pretty fancy with a sewing machine, and as it turns out, making cloth bags is a great scrap buster.

So I started off my New Year by sewing myself fifteen reusable drawstring bags in various sizes: some large enough to hold the equivalent of a box of cereal all the way down to ones small enough to hold one-quarter cup of tea leaves, or like three gummy bears—when I'll use those, I have no idea, but the fabric is so pretty. And now I'm ready to brave Frenco's once more! Side note: I will bring a couple of glass containers for things like oil, shampoo, and cleaners.

To be honest, I'm a little bit terrified, and my lower back lets me know it. *Maybe you should just wait another year,* I tell myself. *You know, in case anyone recognizes you.* But I'm determined to make this experience better than the last, and I'm glad I push myself because *holy crap, they sell brownie mix in bulk! And salted caramel chunks? And detergent?! Wow, this place is so much cooler than I remember.*

I roam the aisles.

*Yes, I will take an entire bag full of dried, unsweetened mango, thank you.*

*Ooh, maybe this month I should learn how to make my own olive oil.*

*I better get a bag full of those, whatever the hell those things are.*

And then BAM!

*It's a good thing I brought my own egg carton. Only $3.99/dozen if I pack them myself? I pay $7.99/dozen at the big store for the exact same brand!*

*I'm never shopping the major chains again!*

When I get home, I dig out all my glass jars, carefully transfer all the contents from the bags, then sit back and enjoy the look of my new pantry. The entire process, from start to finish, feels... uh, I can't believe I'm going there, but... meditative? Like some sort of prayer?

I feel deeply satisfied.

And the best part? I don't have anything to throw away. I just put all my drawstring bags back into my shopping bag and hang them quietly in the hallway closet.

## WINE & ALCOHOL

I'm not a big drinker, but I do enjoy a glass of wine here and there. I'm excited about today's little trip because I'm finally visiting a bulk wine and hard-alcohol store at the other end of the city. You can buy six bottles at a time, reuse them forever, and refill them yourself. It sounds like a mythical place, but my mother-in-law and stepfather-in-law (say that ten times real fast) assure me this is where they go to buy their yearly supply of wine. *Yearly supply of…?*

I park in the lot close to the entrance of the warehouse because as I learned from my first time shopping at Frenco's, glass is heavy. I don't want to have to walk it very far. But as I take a closer look, I notice there are all kinds of carts around with signs noting that it's obligatory to use them. You know—so you don't do something stupid, like break your back *(hey, at least I know to lift with my legs)*.

I load my two twelve-pack cases of empty bottles into a cart—that should last me the week—and make my way into the store. A lady greets me and removes all the previous screw caps and gives me new ones. I don't know if they sanitize the old ones; they could melt them down and recycle them, but they could also throw them out, which isn't zero waste, I know. But it's better than getting all the other crap that comes with a wine purchase in Québec, right? It seems like every home is run rampant with those reusable six-compartment bags which are designed to hold nothing but wine bottles, rendering them completely useless for anything else. Except maybe transporting a collection of giant Matryoshkas, or all that extra-large PVC pipe just lying around the house.

Anyway.

There is a tasting station in the center of the warehouse where you can sample the fifteen or so different wines on tap. Each is contained in a giant metal drum along the outer walls, and each is outfitted with a roll of stickers so you can label the bottles yourself. Since this is zero waste, I won't be using the stickers... *except I better take one of two just in case I take wine to someone's house. That'd look weird if it didn't have a label, right?* I'm off to a bad start.

The first thing I notice is that the wines are significantly less expensive. As in nearly one-half to two-thirds the cost of the individually packaged bottle you'll find at the local SAQ, which is our wine-and-alcohol store here in Québec. I tell you, this zero-waste thing is paying off.

I look over the wines carefully and begin tasting. Because there are fifteen or so, it's no wonder there are signs everywhere warning taste-testers about consumption. I don't need more than a micro-sip myself to determine whether or not I like a wine, so I take a few sips and toss the rest. I guess I'm afraid I'll like them all so much I'll lose all sense of self-control and end up blacked out on the floor under one of the spigots. *Moms. We're such lightweights sometimes.*

Alas, my fears never come to fruition. I find four wines, two chosen by my ex-husband—we are very good friends, but that's an entirely different book—and I fill all two dozen bottles to the very, very top. (They never fill them all the way in bottling plants, and there's probably a good reason for that, but whatever, I'm getting my money's worth.)

Nine dollars per bottle is my average. If I were to buy these pre-packaged I would average $14 per bottle. Zero waste is really tasting good now.

## MEAT

Um. Not much to write here just yet because I'm finishing off all the stuff in my freezer. This might be a month-four kind of thing.*

*I'm leaving this in the book because this is where I was in my thinking early in the project. Interestingly, I unintentionally became a vegetarian at home. Perhaps because I grew exhausted from all the years of eating "Beef. It's what's for dinner." Or perhaps because I thought if I don't have the nerve to kill my own meat in the wild, I shouldn't buy so much of it in the store. Either way, I didn't miss it because I ate meat whenever I attended family dinners or went out to restaurants.

## PERSONAL CARE PRODUCTS

Sometimes I do things out of order because I'm too excited to try something. For Christmas this year, I had this zero-waste book project in mind, and so I thought I'd better ask Santa for bamboo toothbrushes just in case I made the nice list. I found some that are compostable and shipped in bulk. I know I'm not using my own containers to buy them, but who cares! Santa listened and ordered me a bag full, and I gotta say, these things are great! You can't do much with the bristles, besides pluck them out and toss them when you're done with your toothbrush, but the bamboo body is completely compostable or upcycleable. I'm just trying to think of ways one could upcycle them besides the obvious "plant markers" idea. Hand carve them into mini totem poles? Maybe if I save enough of them I could hot glue them together to make a hot pad for the kitchen. Or some sort of abstract piece of art I can give my mom next Christmas. (Moms are not allowed to complain about their child's artwork, so it doesn't have to look good or make any sense.) And anyway, I'm going to have to figure out how to be zero waste next holiday season. I better start brainstorming now.

I think Bea Johnson, who I refer to as my Zero-Waste Goddess, or Zee Dub for short, uses toothbrushes of this nature. But hers are 100 percent compostable because the bristles are probably made from boar hair. Or badger hair. I heard those are great for people with sensitive teeth. I have room to improve, clearly. So I've taken it upon myself to order some miswak sticks. They're 100 percent compostable... because they're an actual stick. From a bush.

To properly use a miswak stick, you chew off the surrounding bark at one end, then chomp on the core until the fibers separate and start to feel like bristles. Then you run the "bristles" around your teeth and mouth in the way you would a regular toothbrush.

One YouTube blogger, edofolks, was a strict twig chewer, even after he moved to the United States, because he felt they cleaned far better than regular toothbrushes. That was, of course, until he discovered an Oral-B electric toothbrush. But still, an Oral-B electric toothbrush couldn't replace the seven mouth-cleaning products a twig could. According to him, one stick could replace gum cleaners, with the little rubbery doodad at the end; those horrible-looking metal toothpicks the dentists use to prod around your mouth searching for cavities; floss; toothbrushes; tongue scrapers; toothpaste; and mouthwash. This is good, because I was wondering what kind of crazy recipe I'd have to research in order to make my own mouthwash. I was hoping I could get away with wine, if I'm honest.

There's more to this whole chewing stick thing, though. I've found numerous quoted studies online that talk about the antibiotic and antiviral properties of certain types of twigs—*actual health benefits*. And there seem to be many! But you know that famous quote by Abe Lincoln going around Facebook: "The problem with quotes on the internet is that it's hard to verify their authenticity." I'm obviously going to have to do some real research.

## REFLECTIONS OF THE MONTH
JANUARY 1, 2016


I visited several stores in and around the neighborhood this month, trying as hard as I could only to buy stuff that didn't come in non-compostable packaging. At shops like Frenco's, it's fairly simple, but in the major grocers, it's nearly impossible. Not because there aren't choices. I can shop some sections of the store like fruits and vegetables, for instance, no problem. It's the *rest* of the store that gives me grief.

I have decided to compare kicking my packaging addiction to the few times I've ever kicked a sugar addiction. The first couple days were great because I was so excited about the real changes I was going to make in my life. Days three and four were the worst—I was cranky, had no patience, and sometimes tore the walls apart looking for chocolate—but by the time day six or seven rolled around, I didn't even crave sugar anymore.

So, it's kinda similar except instead of taking six or seven days, it's probably going to take me *three months because temptation is everywhere!* It pisses me off!

I still find that when I drive by a major grocer, I'm tempted to run in and buy something just for the sake of buying something. I don't need it… and I know I don't need it! But plastic packaging *feels* good. The labels are pretty. The colored inks are so bright. The designs. The branding. The *logos*, my god the logos! And when you see the 20 percent markdown sticker, you feel like it would be stupid *not* to buy whatever is in front of you. Damn those marketing geniuses.

Suffice it to say, I've relapsed a few times. But you know what made me feel ten times worse than buying packaged dinner one night when I was in a hurry because I forgot to thaw something? *All the damn trash.*

I swear, one little bag of groceries produced enough trash to somehow end up in several rooms of my house over the course of three days. Wrappers were on my desk, a small empty box ended up in the dining room, a crinkly plastic cover in the living room…

My tolerance for clutter seems to be diminishing. What

if this zero-waste journey leads me to my ultimate fear… minimalism?

In the meantime, I'm going to unsubscribe from all my online shopping sites like Groupon. That should help, right?

# CHAPTER TWO:
## I'VE GOT WORMS
### FEBRUARY 5, 2016

It's February 5. My kids are sleeping soundly; it's 9:30p.m., and I *should* be going to bed. What am doing instead? Talking to you about composting. My two-o'clock self is slapping the shit out of me right now. I had to slam a double coffee to stave off the fatigue this afternoon, but I'm too excited.

This month was supposed to be about finding zero-waste cosmetics, but I'm moving that to another month because I can't stand the smell of all the rotting food coming from my kitchen. I swear my trash intake dropped by 90 percent last month just because I started shopping with my own containers.

My garbage contains mostly food scraps: banana peels, some cooked chicken, coffee grinds… and I finally had the courage to take it out this morning, but while I was trying to tie my compostable bag in a knot—which is way harder when you're holding your breath, for some reason—I got to wondering why it smelled so bad. Then I wondered when the last time was that I actually took out the trash.

And facepalm.

Nearly two weeks. Two weeks?!

Oh yeah. And I just remembered there's a diaper in the

bottom of the bag somewhere.

I let it get out of hand because the bag wasn't filling up nearly as quickly as before, so I thought *why bother? What's another week going to change? It's winter.*

Let me tell you, if I can smell my garbage now—and I'm not known for my smelling abilities, which is why I never minded diaper changes—it will be three times worse in the hot, unair-conditioned, third-floor-apartment summer.

I needed a solution for my stinky garbage, fast, so I did some research and a couple hours later, BAM! There it was!

Compost!

Of course! Why didn't I think of that earlier?

I googled "compost Montreal" and as it turns out, there are two companies that collect residential compost privately. The city does pick up compost, they just don't do it in *my* neighborhood. Jerks.

The cheapest company could do a pickup for $7.50 per week. It's not much, really. But when you're a single mom, it's a monthly expense of $30 that could be spent on something practical, like Canada's version of the Almond Joy. Or my Netflix account. Something to help me stay sane.

So I decided to call on my crafty side by googling "DIY apartment composting." A plethora of ideas popped up ranging from IKEA hacks, to plastic tubs full of red worms, to my personal favorite, a YouTube video by Lee Gaines called "F**K it...I am Composting! How to Compost If You Live In An Apartment Complex," which basically details Lee Gaines walking through a residential area to a nearby park, where he cleverly deposits his food scraps underneath a bush just off the walking path. Then he walks home.

This guy is a genius. I don't know why I didn't think of that sooner, honestly. But again, it's winter. Maybe I'll try his technique in the summer in some unassuming neighbor's yard. But until then, I need a plan.

The more I think about composting, the more I dig the whole worm idea. And I don't mean that as a pun. I'm serious. My kids want pets, and this could be my answer. We could name them. Or we could name one and I'll pretend they're all the same worm; better the chances of seeing one in the giant bin, right? *Look, honey, there's Bertha the worm! Oh look at that corner of the bin, there she is again!* My two-year-old is either going to be very confused about the speed with which worms travel, or he's going to be more excited than that time he yelled "SPIDER-MAN!" and we actually understood him.

Now, where can I find worms in Montreal? In winter?


## FEBRUARY 10, 2016


Yesterday, I directed a photo shoot for a company I used to work for that sells wholesale Italian women's fashion. The shoot consisted of me, our model, my lovely assistant, a photographer, and a makeup artist I'd never met before. After a super intense morning of photos, we had a break of two and a half hours before we could start shooting at our next location. Being that we were famished, I decided to take the girls to a friend-of-the-family's cafe called Campanelli's on Notre Dame.

After staring at the menu for what seemed like half an hour—why is it so hard to order when you're hungry?!—we finally placed our orders. I tried not to talk about anything remotely zero waste so I wouldn't bore anyone, but I couldn't resist pointing out the fact that Campanelli's hand-stamps their logo on their compostable packaging.

The food arrived, a hot meatball sub for me, since I'm not a model, and we were well into the meal when my phone rang.

It was Beth, the Worm Lady.

I reached out to her on Kijiji, Canada's version of craigslist, a few days earlier because I saw she'd posted an ad about selling red wrigglers in the area, the kind of worms needed for indoor composting.

"Hello, this is Jaren."

"Hi, Jaren, this is Beth from the ad on Kijiji."

"You've got worms!" At the top of my lungs in the middle of the café.

"Yes, yes I do!" she politely giggled.

Beth is retired, but like most retirees I know, she's probably busier than the rest of us. She's got a very kind voice, and I can't wait to meet her in person. I told her I'm bringing my kids to pick up the worms and that we're going to name them. She laughed, we coordinated the pickup, and then she ended the conversation by saying that she's happy to be selling me the worms because "we all need to be doing our part for the earth."

I love this lady. She's not in-your-face about her worm business. She's kind, and by having such a lovely demeanor, I'm officially a convert. I want to compost everything in sight.

So after hanging up the phone, in my newly converted glow, I announced with the same amount of enthusiasm I would have if I found out Celine Dion wanted to be friends with me, that I am driving to NDG to get my worms on Saturday! Then I shrieked with excitement!

Cricket... cricket.

Then I scrambled to put everything into context while our model tried to choke down the rest of her salad. My team acted interested, but I think they were just trying to be nice. Except the photographer—her dad composted with worms when she was growing up and got really excited every time it was time to harvest worm castings, basically worm poop, or "compost."

So I'm shared my excitement with him.

Bertha. Magnus. Book. Those are good names for

worms.

## FEBRUARY 13, 2016

I never got a chance to meet Beth the Worm Lady. My kids and ex-husband did, though. I stayed in the car while they went inside because I got the flu. They said she was very nice and her place didn't even smell wormy. I'm not sure what wormy smells like; I'm trying to image it. But I said if she was composting correctly, then there should be no foul smell whatsoever.

*See? I've been doing my research.* And that makes me an expert in this field now, even though I haven't even built my worm bin yet. But that all starts now!

Armed with Kleenex, my drill, IKEA bins, newspaper—which I picked out of the recycling bin in the entryway of my building, in case you were wondering— food scraps, and a post I found on Pinterest, I'm ready to build the ultimate DIY Worm Bin. A runny nose can't stop me.

This looks like it will be the easiest DIY project I've done in years! It should be illegal not to compost, now that I think about it. Maybe I'm going to write our politicians about this—you know, be single-handedly responsible for climate change reversal in Montreal. I'm going to be a hero.

First steps first, I have to drill holes all around the bin. This is so the worms can breathe. I read that they won't escape so long as their environment isn't too acidic, so I shouldn't be worried about using such a large drill bit. Since I'm going to be the best worm mom ever, I plan to drill more holes than necessary to really show these worms how much I care for them and trust them not to escape. This is how I plan to parent my kids when they're teenagers.

But… it feels like someone—I won't say who (rhymes

with rex gusband)—may have tried to drill a hole through a steel beam with this bit. It's so dull, it takes all my weight to make a hole in the plastic. I could stop what I'm doing and drive all the way to Home Depot to buy a sharp bit—because *that* would take less time—but given how much I'm sweating right now, I think this counts as a workout. So technically, I'm killing two birds with one stone. No way am I drilling extra holes, though.

Now that I'm done, I just have to wet some newspaper, without overwetting it, and layer it with dry newspaper.

And repeat.

And then add food scraps and worms and more newspaper.

*Voilà.* That was easy. Now all I have to do is put my food scraps in one corner of the bin for a week and make sure the environment doesn't get too wet. Then I have to rotate corners every week and occasionally add more dry newspaper for a few months until it's time to harvest the worm castings! (Essentially how it works is that the worms eat all the newspaper and food scraps and poop out compost.) So sometime in May, I'll dump the bin over and be able to gently separate the worms from my very own, home-grown compost! I don't know what I'll do with the compost—maybe give it as a gift to my friends with backyard gardens. Or start a balcony garden. My mind is running wild with ideas.

## FEBRUARY 25, 2016

Good news! The kids are cool with the worms! My son wanted to hold one for a minute, so I let him, but my daughter was more interested in getting back to her dolly kindergarteners, so our first family interaction was somewhat short. Which is fine. I'm feeling protective of the worms because they have a lot of work to do, so I don't want the kids distracting them too much.

## MONTH TWO RECAP:
### FEBRUARY 27, 2016

We eat an extraordinary amount of vegetables, I'm coming to realize. There's no way these worms have time to eat all the scraps we produce. I'm trying to be conscious of how many scraps I'm putting in the compost: cutting as close to the base of the celery stalk as possible; reducing the amount of citrus I consume because I heard worms don't like it; and not eating meat or as much dairy as before because you can't compost those.

I'm changing my ways to appease my worm colony. Or as I discovered online, they're also called a bed, squirm, wriggle, clew, clat, bunch, or knot of worms.

A simple solution would be to start a second worm bin, but my place is so tiny I don't know where I'd put it. The good news is that the bin doesn't smell, but maybe that's because it hasn't had time to really break down. It's only been a couple of weeks.

All I know is that I feel a lot better about myself for having worms. Mother Nature and I are getting to be besties. Maybe we'll get matching tattoos soon.

## SHOPPING WITH MY OWN
## CONTAINERS: UPDATE

You know what comes in a surprising amount of packaging? Gum. And mints. So I've been on the lookout for eco-friendlier manufacturers. There's a company that makes a natural gum that comes in a bar, kind of like chocolate. It's wrapped in one layer of packaging, so it's less offensive than commercial products. When you need some, you break off however much you feel like chewing. And it's really fun to chew, but only for ten to fifteen minutes. After that, it loses all flavor. This is okay because I'm not a marathon chewer to begin with, but I can imagine people who are used to conventional brands might complain about this.

I'm still an irritable shopper. I can't go into a major chain grocer just yet. I get too pissed off and woe-is-me when I see all the packaging. I can't even go to my friends' apartments now.

*I'd love to have that product in my house.*

*No I wouldn't. It's loaded with chemicals. It's probably killing them slowly, and they don't even know it.*

*It smells so good, though.*

*But look at all that waste.*

This is exhausting.

# CHAPTER THREE:
## ZERO-WASTE BEAUTY
### MARCH 2, 2016

I have an issue with some of the more recent, local "zero wasters" I've seen on TV. They're so hard-core they don't wear makeup. Perhaps it's because they're more evolved. You know? Or, maybe, becoming zero waste changed their priorities and they simply no longer see the importance. I don't know. Look, I am a believer in letting anyone live the way they please, but I don't think you'll convince the majority of the population that a zero-waste lifestyle is cool if you look like a troll on television. And it's not their fault! TV lighting is extreme and awfully unkind to the unairbrushed face. And I don't know about you, but most women I know don't feel all that presentable without some sort of makeup product on their visage, anyway. There's a much deeper conversation to be had surrounding all this, of course (WHY SHOULD WE, AS WOMEN, FEEL WE HAVE TO WEAR MAKEUP TO BEGIN WITH?!), but I'm going to end on a shallow note here by telling you that mascara is my minimum. **That's why I'm dedicating month three of my journey to simple, zero-waste body care and makeup solutions.**

But I have a couple of concerns.

Firstly, will they actually work? I've tried my share of

natural recipes over the years, and I have to say that some of them just don't cut it. And I do a fair amount of work in the public eye, so if I want to promote zero waste, I want to do it looking like Gisele Bündchen. I want people to say to themselves, "If she can make her own makeup out of dirt and chia seeds"—or whatever—"I can too."

Secondly, I want to age gracefully. What if, hypothetically speaking, someone—I won't say who, but her name rhymes with that of the author—is *finally* interested in using skin creams containing anti-aging ingredients like collagen and Retin-A, and god knows what else they advertise? Is there a homemade equivalent for wrinkle prevention?

I've toyed with the idea of making my own makeup, like actual cosmetics and not just skin creams, for several years and have tried quite a few recipes up to this point. Why? There are plenty of eco-companies out there who make organic makeup already. Surely if they care so much about supplying organic ingredients, they care enough to limit the amount of garbage their products produce. Right? But these ideas don't necessarily go hand in hand.

Take, for example, the fact that there are a number of brands who use the word "organic" on their packaging strictly to make a sale. As in "Made with Organic Ingredients." Flip the package over and you might discover that only 10 percent of the ingredients are organic. False advertising? Yes and no. They're being honest that only 10 percent of the ingredients are organic. But they're counting on us, their consumers, to focus on the word "organic" itself, probably so we'll feel better about buying their product over their not-so-much-better competition. This is where, as a consumer, I have learned to take more responsibility.

But it's not so obvious when it comes to packaging. I've worked for companies who advertise their products as being eco-friendly just to attract a different audience to their brand. Were they concerned about the environment in the least? Not that I could tell.

My point is that if there's a way to make my own cosmetics in a way that makes me feel good, look good, and have less impact on the environment, why not try it? This is where I enlist the help of Marie, from humblebeeandme.com.

I discovered Marie's blog online several months ago and have become obsessed. Here is a woman who has found a homemade solution for nearly every beauty product I've ever imagined. I use the term "I" here, because I am not someone who knows makeup inside and out; I shop at Sephora maybe once a year, if I'm lucky. Back to Marie, though. She's just penned a book called *Make It Up*, which features insane cosmetic recipes you can make in your kitchen, I'm told.

Why would she do that? I set up an interview to find out.

Marie lives in Calgary, and she's skyping from the living room of her house. She's calm and approachable, and I'm a nervous mess. I've never interviewed anyone before—I mean formally—and I only have thirty minutes, so I start by telling her about this zero-waste book project. She tells me about her book, which is coming out in September, and before we know it, we find our groove. I start throwing questions at her right and left.

*What got you interested in making cosmetics?*
*Can you really make mascara from scratch?*
*What about face primer?*

"Primer. That was the hardest part. I tried so many recipes," she says, shaking her head. For those of you who don't know much about makeup and know more about, say, construction, a *face primer* does the same thing a paint primer does. It gets whatever you paint on it afterward to stick. For a long time.

"You can do pretty much anything in this primer and your makeup will stay on," she assures. "I know because I put my recipes through rigorous testing."

This is how she explains her testing process to me. After formulating a new homemade cosmetic, she would apply it in the morning, work during the day, go do hot yoga for an hour, and she might follow that up by going out dancing with friends. If the makeup was still on her face the next morning, then she knew she was getting somewhere. Her recipes sound so strong I wonder how easy it is to get them off your face. Probably need mineral spirits or something.

So just how did she get into this business? Turns out she and a friend were horrified when they discovered all the toxic ingredients in their makeup products years ago while attending university. A lover of cooking and reverse-engineering recipes, she decided to try making her own cosmetics. But, like me, she discovered most of the recipes out there just weren't up to Sephora-like standards, so she spent years reformulating and retesting until she was satisfied.

Her love of design and marketing lead her to create humblebeeandme.com. She is very engaged with her audience, so it's no wonder her first book deal didn't take long. She poured everything into it, including extensive research. And by the sound of it, probably more than I'm willing to do for this project.

One thing I found surprising is that she's a meat-loving vegetarian. Like me, she loves a good steak. But she doesn't eat it because of the carbon footprint. And in the same breath she says when it comes to making her own soaps, she prefers to use beef tallow or pig lard over palm oil, a common ingredient. Hypocritical? I'll let you decide.

"Look, I'm using the discarded fat of animals that have already been slaughtered and that will otherwise rot and go to waste. And the fact is, palm oil harvesting is wiping out wildlife habitats. So when people complain that I'm using the fat of animals in my soaps, I have to ask... what's worse?"

The takeaway here? Don't take things at face value. Just because a company is advertising they're selling a green or eco product doesn't mean they're not using ingredients that are causing harm to the environment. We have to pick our poison.

We change the subject. When asked if I want to see her collection of eye shadows, I say *yes*, thinking she'll show me a few baby-food jars full of earthy powders that are basically just ground-up root vegetables, cinnamon, or cocoa powder. You know, something I could make.

Laptop in hand, she runs upstairs to her bathroom and reveals a collection of jaw-droppingly rich, pigmented eye colors. She shows me how she applies them, and near as I can tell, they rival anything I've seen in an advertisement for MAC. She shows me several eyeliners ranging in color from black to bright metallic teal and burgundy. *And the super-coveted primer.* Again, she reiterates the fact that you can do hot yoga, party, and sleep in this stuff and your makeup won't come off. I ask her about making mascara—my crutch.

"I saw a recipe on Pinterest that said I could mix oil, water, and charcoal. But that sounds about as ridiculous as using a Sharpie," I say. "Do you have a recipe?"

"No emulsifier? Who posted that? I have a great recipe for mascara, but that's one product that is impossible to make with basic kitchen ingredients."

I feel disappointed. How can I make my own line of skin products zero waste if I have to send away for some special waxes and products I can't pronounce? But Marie assures me most of the companies she buys her products from are eco-conscious. And if you commit to making your own products and buying ingredients in bulk, then does it offset the onetime shipping? We pause.

"I didn't just get into the business of making my own cosmetics to be green. I like the idea that if my favorite product is discontinued, I can just make it myself. I'm not limited." And she can make it a heck of a lot cheaper.

We continue talking for a while about kombucha—she gives me a recipe—and then I tell her about my plans to try soap making.

"I really wanna make goat's milk soap," I announce. "I just love the natural color, and my friend made some for me a few years ago, and they changed my life. They can't be that hard to make."

Pause.

"That's pretty advanced. Why don't you try something easier? I have an all-in-one bar that's great for first-time soap makers. I use it as my shampoo, body bar, hand bar, everything. Way easier than messing with milk bases. For a beginner, I mean."

Shampoo, body, hand, everything? Jeez. If I could make an all-in-one bar, I could stop buying all those products separately. One batch would last me a couple of years, I bet. That seems pretty zero waste to me. But I really wanna try making goat's milk soap. My inner hipster thinks it's SUCH a good idea, and I'm good at reading recipes and following instructions. How hard can it be? Plus, I'm a little daring when it comes to this kind of thing, so I decide to ignore her advice and try it anyway. I think she realizes this, because she adds, "Be sure you don't scald your milk. You can freeze it in cubes and mix that with your lye." I read that on a soap-making blog earlier in the week, so I feel confident my first attempt at this will grant me bragging rights.

It's time to hang up. We've been skyping for two and half hours! Since her book won't be out for another six months*, I have to wait to try her more advanced cosmetic recipes like eye shadows, liners and foundation. In the meantime, I'll just have to recount my experiences thus far with household recipes. Perhaps you'll learn from my mistakes.

\* Marie Rayma's book Make It Up: The Essential Guide to DIY Makeup and Skin Care released December 26, 2016, through Running Press

# SIMPLE RECIPES

## DEODORANT

When I was probably twelve or so, I remember once being in the bathroom with my sister, Josie, watching my mom put on makeup and get dressed after her morning shower. I don't know if she was in a bad mood, if her nursing studies were getting to her, or if Josie and I were just being little brats that day, but I remember her telling us that deodorant had aluminum in it and that it would probably cause cancer. Josie and I were shocked.

"Then why are you still using it?!"

Because she had to, for work.

"You're going to die?"

"Yes, of course. Maybe from this. Who knows," she quipped.

Now that I'm a mom, I can only imagine she was trying to get us back for not doing the dishes or something. She was probably smiling the whole time, in her head.

I was so traumatized by that moment, however, that I didn't sleep well for weeks afterward. I knew I didn't like deodorant, even though it smelled pretty and made me feel like a proper teenager. But I didn't have any better alternative, and I wasn't about to scare the boys away with my stinky pits. So as an adult, I decided to find a different solution. There were plenty!

The stone.

*Didn't work for me.*

The glycerin deodorant.

*Didn't work for me.*

Alcohol on a swab to kill the armpit bacteria.

*Gross. Nuh-uh. What else?*

Then I found a girl on Etsy who made and sold her own recipe from her home in Florida. She formulated it to work in the intensely humid heat. The reviews were out of this world. Surely if it worked for her it would work for me—*and it did*. It smelled beautiful and came in a tin and was called KP's Pit Paste. As of a few years ago she stopped making the product. I was devastated.

*What do I do? Can I recreate it?*

So I dug around and was surprised to find she had an ingredient list on one of the tins she sent.

*If she can make it, I can make it.*

After several attempts, I discovered an even simpler recipe, which used equal parts arrowroot powder and baking soda, mixed with coconut oil to the desired consistency. If I'm feeling extra fun, I can add some essential oils. But I often don't.

I swear by this recipe and have been using it for years. I even got the ex-husband on board. (He has to wear it for tae kwon do practice because it's the only deodorant strong enough to fight back. Hahaha, get it?) The best part about this recipe is that the ingredients are almost always in my house.

## TOOTHPASTE

Fluoride or no fluoride?

This is a big question. The internet is divided. So I switch back and forth. You know, cut my chances of dying in half... or better my chances of strengthening my teeth by 50 percent. I don't really know. But I like the idea of trying to create my own toothpaste, and I've tried many recipes.

I first started out with the whole baking soda and water on a toothbrush thing. No way my kids were going to stick with that. So I tried a jarred paste from a company here in Montreal. That was pretty darn tasty, and I have all the ingredients listed on the label—maybe I'll try to recreate it. I just need to improve the texture because my kids are picky.

I then tried a DIY recipe for an equivalent to Earth Paste, a toothpaste made with only five ingredients: water,

Redmond clay, real salt, xylitol, and essential oils. It worked, I'll say that much. It takes a minute to get used to the flavor and texture (and the California Prop65 Cancer warning), but Earth Paste is endorsed by a few dentists, according to their website, so I decided that was enough to get me through a tube of it. Still, I wanted other options, so I looked up a recipe for tooth *powder*.

The tooth powder recipe I tried involved xylitol and some other stuff. It was clay-based and left my mouth feeling very clean, but also a little muddy. It was easily fixed by rinsing with a tall glass of water afterward, which I always do anyway because the water feels colder when your mouth is burning from peppermint oil. My kids weren't big fans, however. Still? Gosh they're hard to convince. So, I tried talking up tooth tabs as a possible solution.

There are a few recipes for tooth tabs online. They are small, single-serving portions of tooth cleaner that become activated with a wet toothbrush or your own saliva, basically. I have this really great silicone hot pad, which features a honeycomb pattern, so clever ol' me decided to try pressing a batch of homemade paste into the mold and letting it dry for several hours. Then I flipped the pad over and popped all the tiny tooth tabs out. It worked!

After they dried completely, I put them into a little glass jar in my bathroom. *Perfectly portioned so you never have to worry about putting too much on your brush.* The only thing I didn't like about these tabs is that you really need to make sure no moisture gets inside the jar. Otherwise they'll stick together. And mold, would be my guess. Still, my kids hated them.

Recently I gave up the search for the perfect toothpaste recipe and tried a banana toothpaste sold in bulk at a new zero-waste shop here in Montreal. Finally, the kids are happy, which makes me happy. I'm having trouble convincing myself I don't have to make everything from scratch for this project, though.

## MOUTHWASH

Sweet hallelujah, I can make my own mouthwash!
Vodka.

No, actually I found a really tasty recipe online, so for my ex's birthday, I made him an all-natural care package: tooth powder, the one I liked, and homemade mouthwash. Mostly I made it in the hope that if we ever had a dramatic fight I could shout something clever like *"Nothin' but lies comin' out of your dirty, rotten mouth! And to think, you have no excuse! I made you mouthwash!"*

That'll never happen.

The homemade mouthwash recipe I like most contains distilled water, aloe vera, baking soda, xylitol, and essential oils. And when you use it, your mouth feels... pretty. That's the only word I can think of to describe the feeling. Clean, sure. But it's more than that. It's fresh, but not burning. Much more pleasant than Listerine, and a hell of a lot cheaper.

## EYELINER

My interest in kohl eyeliner started when ZeeDub showed off her makeup routine in one of her videos. It's very minimalist. She makes her kohl out of almonds and applies it to her eye line, as is done in many parts of the world. I thought this could be a good option for me. *If everybody else can do this, I can too.* So I googled some recipes, chose the simplest one, and went to town. How hard could it be?

It's very easy, actually. It would have been a more enjoyable experience had I made it in a kitchen with a vented hood, because I set the fire alarm off twice. But sure as heck, blackened almonds go onto the skin very much like a black eyeliner, in terms of color. I didn't have a very good method for applying this stuff, which is why I didn't stick with it. I looked in all kinds of stores for those kohl pots with the metal wand inside. When I finally bought one, I discovered the wand had been bent, so applying kohl without destroying my corneas would have been impossible. Eventually, I looked into buying a package of kohl in bulk, which came with a traditional kohl container and wand. But many kohls seem to be made of ash and other compounds that could possibly contain heavy metals. Even if it weren't 100 percent true, I decided to look for a different solution.

I found a couple of recipes online for eyeliner and mascara using charcoal and/or black clay. They did warn that if the mixture got into the eye, however, it could burn. What the...? That's ridiculous! Why would you paint your eyes with something that could likely burn them? But we all know what I did. I tried it anyway. Not so bad, I thought when I applied it. It seemed to dry nicely. Maybe this could work. But five minutes later I was laughing so hard about something I read online, I started to tear up, which moistened the mixture and sucked it into my eyeballs.

"HOLY SHIT! THEY'RE ON FIRE!"

It's amazing, my sense of direction. I was able to find the bathroom sink in my house with my eyes completely closed in under five seconds without running into a wall or running over my children.

I can't wait until Marie's book comes out so I can try her eyeliner recipe.

## PORE CLEANSING MASK

Now that I had all this charcoal and clay left over from my failed eyeliner experiment, I needed to figure out a way to use it. A Pinterest post popped up with a two-ingredient mask that was guaranteed to suck all the living yuck out of my pores. So I decided to try it. (I had a fancy dinner to attend that night, so I wanted to show up looking fresh.)

Now… I should have been a little curious when I saw the list of ingredients. Or maybe I should have used my past mascara experience to guide me toward a different recipe, but as we all know, *if it's got a thousand likes on the internet, it must be good.* So I got busy.

I mixed up equal parts *white glue* and *charcoal. Yeah, yeah, I know.* Then I applied a thick layer all over my face. I realized, while trying to wash it off my hands, that this stuff is real hard to get off. I had to use some oil and lots of scrubbing, which left my hands very red.

Uh-oh.

I realized at this point I had two options: A) frantically try to remove the mask while simultaneously turning all my towels black, using up an entire container of coconut oil, and rubbing the first three layers of my skin off; or B) let it dry, as the recipe says to do, then pull the whole thing off in one go. Maybe it won't leave too much charcoal behind.

I decided to go with option B. I figured I'd better let it get *really* dry, so I left it on for thirty minutes instead of fifteen. But I started to sense there might be a problem when my ex-husband showed up to pick up a bag of clothes for the kids and could barely contain himself when he saw my face.

"Are you okay?" he giggled. I ran to the bathroom mirror to find out.

Lord, almighty! I looked like one of those women addicted to plastic surgery.

Where the glue dried, the mask contracted heavily, forcing all the blood in my face to my lips, since they were the only part exposed. My forehead seemed to have migrated a full inch, and when I tried yelling *"OMG!"* my face refused to move. I started pulling frantically at the mask. I'd humiliated myself enough already!

The thing about dried glue/charcoal is that it acts like a wax. So, while it *may* have cleaned my pores, it literally pulled all the baby hairs off my face, leaving me with red patches all over. And I still had to scrub off the remaining charcoal. My face looked terrible, but it was going to be okay, right? I still had four hours to heal before the fancy dinner. How could I have forgotten Hollywood's number one rule: don't get a facial the day of an event.

Let's just say it took a full twenty-four hours for my face to recover. I wore a lot of foundation that night and constantly checked myself in the bathroom mirror for red patches. I'm sticking to my bentonite clay masks, thank you very much.

## BENTONITE CLAY MASKS

I bought a jar of bentonite clay years ago at the recommendation of an actress who swore by the stuff. It was the end-all in the search for the perfect face mask, she said. You mix a little of this stuff with water, apply it to your face, then let it dry for fifteen minutes or so. I've always had bentonite clay on hand and never had any problems with it, myself. I find it's a common ingredient in a lot of zero-waste recipes because it's easy to buy in bulk, and it seems to be pretty versatile.

## GHASSOUL / RHASSOUL CLAY

If you haven't tried ghassoul clay before, it's worth looking into. I can find it in bulk in Montreal, and I simply mix it with water to form a thin paste. I rub it into my scalp and hair and let it sit for a few minutes while I shave, and then I rinse it out. I don't even need to use a conditioner afterward, and brushing my hair with a fine-tooth comb is ridiculously easy. I like to comb it into whatever style I want before it dries, though, because when it does, it's not as easy to comb, for me anyway. But my hair never looks greasy when I use this method, which is one of the reasons I continue to do so.

The *only* reason I don't use it all the time is because I'm a little worried about buildup in my pipes. I haven't done any research, but I know clay can build up unless you use a lot of water to flush it out, and I'm trying to reduce my water consumption as well. So. I limit myself to using this method once every couple weeks.

## SHAMPOO BARS

Marie has a recipe for an all-in-one bar, which she uses to wash her hair. I didn't believe her at first. Her hair was very long for our interview, and my face probably spent a good minute taking up her entire screen, squinting in concentration trying to examine it through the webcam. It looked beautiful, like in those Pantene commercials. Nothing at all like mine when I tried washing my hair with store-bought soap bars. I contacted her later to ask why, and she helped me trouble shoot. I probably needed to use a different bar because the pH of the soap I used was likely too high. Perhaps this is a bit too technical for me.

I love the idea of shampoo bars, though. Even more than regular shampoos. With shampoo bars, you use only what you need, the bars dry afterward, and you can pack them with you anywhere. This makes traveling by air especially stress-free if you're trying to fit all your liquids into that clear Ziplock which I *swear* the TSA keeps shrinking. If I could make Marie's all-in-one soap bars, and if they worked for my hair, I'd only have to make one batch every couple of years. Imagine all the bottles I'd save!

## BAKING SODA AND VINEGAR

Baking soda and vinegar as shampoo and conditioner were interesting, to say the least. No, my hair never smelled like vinegar. But I did learn very quickly that when you rinse your scalp with vinegar, it's a good idea to close your eyes. I learned how often I shampoo with my eyes open during that experiment. It's a wonder I haven't gone blind by now.

I sometimes use this method when I'm running low on shampoo. But I haven't found the right way to use it long term without making my scalp itch. I must not have the balance right.

## COMMERCIAL SHAMPOOS

I realize most people don't have the time or interest in trying many of these alternative ways of shampooing. Even I don't feel like making my own *everything* all the time. So I try to support local, organic companies who do make shampoos and conditioners—and in Montreal there are thankfully quite a few.

## DRY SHAMPOO

Using cornstarch for dry shampoo was one of the first and is probably the friendliest of my zero-waste recipes. I can buy it at several bulk grocers here in Montreal, and paired with my boar's-hair brush, this stuff works wonders! Just shake it all over your head, wait five minutes, and then brush, brush, brush. Oil be gone!

## BOAR'S-HAIR BRUSH

Luckily these brushes don't come in much of any packaging at most health-food stores. I had one of these growing up and remember loving the way it made my hair feel. I could brush the strands of my hair so smooth, you could run rosin on them and play a violin. I recently bought one to replace my old plastic brush.

I'd forgotten how smooth they made my hair feel—I guess from pulling the natural oils from the scalp down the hair shaft in a more evenly distributed way.

Then I tried drying my hair with one. NOTE TO

SELF: Hot hair dryers burn boar's hair. So either dry your hair on a low heat setting or rotate your brush often, otherwise your bathroom is likely to start smelling like you're at a cattle branding. Unfortunate incident, yes. But this has not prevented me from loving this brush and continuing to swear by it.

## FACIAL TONERS

Glycerin and rose water. I didn't expect how much I would like this "lotion." These two simple ingredients, together, have been a staple in my makeup routine for a few years now because they seem to do a better job of making my skin feel hydrated than many of the fancy products I've tried from Sephora. The other bonus about using this combination of ingredients is that it tastes sweet.

## MONTH THREE RECAP:
### MARCH 28, 2016

Shopping is getting easier!

I feel like I may have had a breakthrough. The frustration seems to be gone. I think it might have to do with the fact that I'm not getting shopping ads in my email and I'm distracting myself with all these new fun discoveries, like learning how to make almond milk from scratch. If people knew how easy it was, they wouldn't buy it. I'm going to tell you right now exactly how I do it so you can try it at home this week.

The night before, I soak one cup of almonds in a bowl of water. The next morning, I drain them, pop them in the blender, and fill the blender ¾ to the top with water. Then I blend for a minute or so. After that, I pour the blended mix into a sieve above a bowl to strain out the pulp. It tastes better than the store-bought version! Add some honey or agave if you want a sweeter version, or drink it as is! I transfer the contents into a glass jar and keep it in my fridge.

Now go make some. You won't regret it. Unless you have an allergy to almonds, in which case, forget I said anything.

Know what else I discovered this month?

- How to make refried beans from dried black beans and beer
- How to make whipped cream using aquafaba, which comes from cooking chickpeas and making a reduction from the water left behind
- How to grow sprouts!

Pretty soon I'm going to stop shaving my armpits and let my leg hair grow a foot long. It's the next logical step, amiright?

On the composting front, I had a minor setback. We—me and the kids—were blowing through vegetables so quickly the worms were having a tough time keeping up. So, I read online that if you want to help them out, you should blend all your food scraps into a pulp and pour it into your compost.

I did that.

And I broke my blender.

The new one came in a lot of packaging. I could have unboxed it right there and left the store without it all, but I felt that would be rude, and anyway *what if I need the box later, in case the blender needs to be repaired?* Gosh. So many things to think about when you're trying to reduce your waste.

My new blender is a dream, though. I'm not blending food scraps so much; I'm just trying to be conscientious about how much food I waste. Buying less and using it before it rots is my main solution. Planning my meals a week before is also helping.

The thing I like most about composting right now is that my apartment no longer smells like the vinegar solution I used to get the smell of cigarette smoke out of my walls when I moved in last year. Instead it smells... earthy. Feels like Mother Earth is holding my hand.

# CHAPTER FOUR:
## ZERO WASTE INTERNATIONAL

I haven't told any of my friends about this zero-waste project yet, just my immediate family and a business colleague. I'm afraid they'll think I've gone off the deep end, so I'll wait until month six to tell them. This way we'll all know if I'm truly serious or if this is another one of my little "dreamer projects."

This month, I'm traveling to Moscow for an EDM (electronic dance music) gig where I will sing for a DJ and a small crowd of around two thousand people. I've decided I'm going to try to make my trip as zero waste as possible.

The biggest challenge I have in prepping for a show, primarily, isn't practicing or getting my voice in shape; it's finding the right outfit for the performance. This part is such a drag for me that I've almost canceled shows mid-travel due to panic attacks. I guess I'm afraid to look stupid on stage? I can't explain it. One minute I'm okay, the next I'm freaking out. I just wish I had a stylist to take care of this stuff for me. It's exhausting being your own publicist, writer, salesperson, photographer, and makeup artist as it is. So, this time around I'm giving myself two weeks before the show to figure out what in the hell I'm wearing.

Now I don't know, but I think all this focus on zero waste is rewiring my brain. I care about what I'll wear on stage, but I also don't care now. Does that make any lick of sense?

Since I have ridiculously expensive taste in fashion, I tend to have to make what I want to wear for public events from scratch. Like my front-pleated crossover pants, which are considered high fashion and a bit androgynous. I designed them myself two years ago to be one size fits all, and to be worn in about six different ways. They're a dark green snake or panther print—I can't really tell—and they include a matching belt. Will these work for my show?

*This looks fine*, I tell myself. *Now I just have to find a top.*

Three years ago, I started this whole *use my life as an experiment* thing with the decision not to buy myself any new clothing for an entire year. In my defense, I think I was still breastfeeding at the time, so my hormones were making my brain all wonky. But I stuck to three rules: I could thrift, I could accept clothes as gifts (or borrow), and socks and underwear were the only items I could buy new.

The entire experience was so successful I continued for another six months before I broke down and bought three T-shirts from H&M. Not nearly as rewarding as I thought it would be. But, by then, I had rediscovered my passion for thrifting, which I realize now is probably an addiction.

Anyway, all this to say I *always* find what I want at Value Village. So that's where I'm going to go hunting for the top to this outfit.

Two days later, I'm flipping through the dress section of Value Village. Some people donate some really weird things. I hate wearing dresses, so I'm not even sure why I'm in this section, but my gut is telling me I'm going to strike gold soon. I'd better—I only have a week to find something, and I don't have much free time to keep digging around.

*And there it is, folks!* I knew I'd find it! *IT* is a long black tank dress with slits up to the waist on both sides. This will go well with my pants. The front can be tied to one side, so it won't cover the crossover pleat.

I think.

*What if this is actually the stupidest outfit ever and I have no sense of judgment?*

*What if people hate it so much they stop liking my music?*

*It's getting real hot in here... when was the last time I ate? Gosh. I always get hangry when I shop.*

I return home and rip through my closet like a tornado trying on the same four tops in different combinations with my pants. Eventually, I settle on a black strapless bra, the black tank, my pants, and some sneakers which were likely made by a twelve-year-old and contain lead. That's not funny because it's not funny. Because it's probably true. My friends work in the shoe industry and tell me horror stories. I hate buying fast-fashion. I can see the faces of the people sewing these shoes together: masks over their faces to lessen the sting of the chemicals used in the factory, working long hours for pennies on the dollar...

But, hey. My outfit is on point.

*Sigh* I hate the world sometimes.

Now I just have to pack everything I'll need to make this trip zero waste.

Okay, so flying zero waste is a little harder than I imagined. Not in terms of finding restaurants or coffee

shops in airports to refill my travel coffee mug, per se.
More in that if you want to drink water, you cannot refuse
to take or buy a water bottle. There is one reason for this.
You could get sick if you drink from the tap, even at the
hotel, I'm told. So I don't argue. I hate being sick in other
countries.

My flight was okay. I was able to bring crackers on the
plane in my own containers. But obviously you can't bring
real food like fruit, veggies, meats, or dairy, so I made sure
to stuff myself before leaving for the airport. This way I
wouldn't be tempted by those little pretzel packets on the
plane. Of course, the minute I found my seat, that's all I
wanted to eat. It's like my stomach is a toddler.

I ate an in-flight meal and didn't feel too bad about it
because A) it's early in my zero-waste transition—I'm a
newbie, so I'm allowed, B) the dishes they used for serving
food on this flight were *obviously* reusable; my ignorant self
is assuming they will be sent straight to recycling after we
all deboard the plane, right...? and C) I'm not holding out
on eating for eight hours.

Look, when it's just me, I'll give it the ol' college try,
and I did. But you better believe if my kids are in the
picture and they're legitimately hungry and not just
whining for a candy, I don't care if food is wrapped in
thirteen layers of plastic. I'm going to make sure they eat.

So I ate that very average in-flight meal and licked my
fingers. Even though the kids weren't even with me.

I requested to fly in a day early to give my voice some
rest, and to stay an extra day so I could rest before flying
home. Years of spending twenty-four hours in a country
that took thirty-six hours each direction to reach taught me
this. This gives me exactly one day to run around Moscow.
I'm not hitting up the Kremlin like I did the first time, or
even any museums. Instead, I've decided to do something
far more dangerous for anyone trying to become zero
waste.

I'm hitting up the brand-new mall!

What could I possibly buy in Moscow zero waste? Well, this is a two-part mission. One is to find my daughter some tights because hers are all worn and have holes in them. Maybe I can find some with little Matryoshkas on them. The second reason is because during the trip, my gross old backpack got a hole in the top that I can't repair and I need a new one. So my driver, Pavel, recommends we go to the nearest mall, which also happens to be the largest in Moscow.

Now, I'm American. I know what "big" means. We have Walmarts and Costcos. Big is big. But this structure rivals anything I've ever seen.

This mall is probably a mile long. It's only four stories tall, but right in the middle, you'll find a giant aquarium, an ice rink, and several playgrounds for children. You can even rent little furry animal cars to ride around on with your kids. Heck, at one point I see mini-cars driving around with babies in them. Alone. I'm about to have a heart attack when I realize their fathers are off to the side using remote controls to steer them clear of other newborns, alone, in remote controlled cars.

This is nutty. Forget the historical landmarks, I'm bringing my kids here next time we visit.

I must point out that one of the things that makes this mall stand out, besides its sheer size, is the fact that the stores are all grouped together. Men's clothing in one area, women's in another, kids' gear on the fourth floor, outdoor gear shops on another floor... I mean some serious planning went into this mall. There is no running around like a headless chicken. Why can't they design malls like this in America?!

So it doesn't take long at all to find tights for my five-year-old *without much packaging*. Or brightly colored underwear for my three-year-old. But when I ask my driver/translator, Pavel, to request at checkout that the cashier *not* give me a plastic bag because I can carry everything in my own backpack, they completely ignore me and give me a bag anyway. The takeaway here is never argue with a Russian in Russia. I try anyway in several other shops, in case I didn't learn my lesson the first few times, to no avail.

Now before you think I went around buying a bunch of frivolous "crap," let me tell you that in fact, I did not. I bought all-natural hemp soap for my family, packaged in compostable brown paper bags, a paper wallet for my baby's daddy, and an extremely well-designed, well-made, better-last-me-twenty-years backpack from Patagonia. In burgundy with a cool zipper pocket on the very top.

Success.

## 24 HOURS LATER

Oh my god. I'm at the airport in Moscow writing this, and the crew just got here for our Air Swiss flight. Forget hot air hostesses. Looks like we have the world's hottest air host. I need to think of a few excuses to use my call button. Zero-waste excuses. Perhaps: "Could you refill my coffee mug?" or "Do you have any of those little cookies in the back in those cute little packages? I don't eat those. I'm against packaging now." That'll go over well, I'm sure.

The thing about Russia I've noticed during this trip is that many of the women here are model-gorgeous. I know that sounds like a hasty generalization, but when Pavel showed me pictures of his girlfriend, I asked, "What is she, a model?" to which he replied very straight-faced, "No, she's Russian girl." Good answer. I'd feel a little down comparing myself to these gals, but all this trash talk is providing me with a fair amount of distraction.

My flight from Moscow to Geneva is quite smooth.

Flying into Geneva's airport is a bit like flying into a mythical fairy-tale land, but you're not crazy because it's real. There are castles on the mountainsides, gorgeous milk cows that probably sing instead of moo, and perfectly snow-capped mountains.

While I'm at the airport, I can't help but notice the sheer amount of watch advertisements, which gets me thinking. Maybe I should invest in a mechanical wind-up watch. After all, a watch without batteries would significantly reduce the amount of battery waste we produce. And battery waste is both toxic and super gross. So I make the rounds.

I soon discover there is no such thing as an affordable watch if you're a single mom operating in Canadian dollars during an economic crisis. The Canadian dollar is shit these days—$1.33 Canadian to $1 American at the time of this writing—which means that the cute little 250 € watch I thought could pass as affordable is actually $366.12 CAD. Nope. What I should be doing is scanning the thrift stores in Montreal. They always have wind-up watches; you just have to find a style that doesn't look completely archaic. Homework for when I get back.

# CHAPTER FIVE:
## ZERO-WASTE SOAP
### MAY 3, 2016

Finally, it's here! The month where I try my hand at making soap from scratch! I could just buy it in bulk because it's sold everywhere in Montreal without packaging. But I really want to understand what goes into the process. Also, I think they'd make great zero-waste gifts for the holidays this year.

Remember how I told Marie, the author of *Make It Up*, that I was going to try making goat's milk soap as my first attempt? Remember how she suggested I try a beginner's recipe instead?

Well, the joke was on both of us.

There's this great little soap, candle, and cosmetic supply store in Little Italy, here in Montreal. I won't say the name, because I'm a little pissed off at them at the moment. They really need to tighten up their online order system—what are we in, the dark ages?!—but if you have time to physically go there, it's worth it.

After doing some light research and talking with Marie, I made a list of ingredients I would need for this goat's milk extravaganza. From now on, I would never have to go to a store and buy health care products full of chemicals like SLS (sodium lauryl sulfate), a surfactant generally viewed by the green world as pretty nasty, nor would I have to bring home all the packaging it comes in. I would be able to make everything at home from scratch. And the good news is, nearly all these raw materials come in packaging I can repurpose or refill.

So, I made my way through the aisles and tried my best to identify all the different things I'd need: citric acid—which up until this point sounded like I could make myself at home using a lemon and a bottle of vinegar (turns out I was wrong)—washing soda, lye, oils, lard, colored micas, and borax, not to be confused with the Lorax. I grabbed the cheapest version of everything. My father's genes are strong.

One thing I'm quite proud of is my ability to figure out recipe substitutions. For example: if I run out of coffee creamer, I'll sometimes put a dollop of yogurt in my brew. If I plug my nose really hard, I can't tell the difference. But you can't cheat or substitute very much when it comes to soap making. It's such an exact process there are online calculators dedicated to helping you figure out all the ingredients in their exact proportions and weights. It's confusing in the beginning, and you don't want to be confused when you're trying to make soap. One of a few things could happen: you could create a soap that burns your skin, one that looks ridiculous because your temperatures were off, or you could lose an entire batch because the mixture never reached a good trace, which I'll explain in a minute. All costly mistakes, let me tell you.

Why am I so hell-bent on making goat's milk soap? My friend Jana, who raises her kids in Wyoming on a farm and remains my prairie homesteading superhero, made goat's milk soap several years ago and gifted me a bag full. These things were the most hydrating, lathering… it was like washing with a bar of lotion! I couldn't get over how good my skin felt using them. That's what fueled my desire to try making them in the first place. So, I scoured the soap-making blogs again and again to make sure I'd be able to ace the recipe on the first try.

The advice Marie gave me appeared over and over again. *Freeze your already measured-out goat's milk before mixing it with the lye.* This way it doesn't scald and stink. It'll just smell kind of "goaty." Seems easy to me.

At home, in my kitchen lab, I measure out all of my ingredients, calculate them to a T, and combine the oils and the lye mixture at the right temperatures and time. But for some reason, it takes about thirty minutes longer than expected to reach *trace*.

In soap speak, *trace* occurs when the combination of all the hot oils, fats, water, and lye go from being a liquid to more of a custard-type consistency. This is necessary for the chemical process, which turns the very caustic lye into something we all want to rub on our skin, to occur.

I'm just not having any luck with kitchen appliances. First, my blender breaks trying to mulch up food scraps for my worms, and now my hand mixer threatens to burn out! I have to cool it off three times, but when I finally reach trace, I'm overjoyed! I can't wait to show Marie my soaps tomorrow after I take them out of their mold.

I can barely sleep I'm so excited.

The next morning I'm counting down the minutes. Typically, soap bars need to cure for at least twelve hours before you make any attempt to remove them. Better still if you can wait twenty-four hours, but that ain't going to happen. I know myself.

Just to be sure, though, I google "can I remove soap bars sooner than 24 hours?" The consensus is yes.

But for some reason the molds are full of goop. My soap didn't cure.

Wait.

What?

WHY?! I did everything right!

After spending thirty minutes re-*tracing* my steps—get it, soap makers?!—I figure I probably didn't wait long enough for my oils to cool. When I mixed them, they were one degree off. One degree!

So, I decide to try again. But I'll have to wait because the kids are with me the next four days, and there's no way I'm making soap around them. (You have to have a healthy respect for lye. You have to protect your eyes and skin because it *will* burn. I read that I should keep a gallon of vinegar nearby just in case, so I have it ready to go every time.)

I love my kids, but this is agony. I'm dying to make my goat's milk bars.

## MAY 9, 2016

Finally, the big day for attempt number two is here! I make sure everything is done as close to perfect as possible. There's no way I'm going to fail again.

But the *same* thing happens!

"WHAT THE HELL?!" I shout. "I just blew like $30 of raw materials! Had this worked, I'd have been able to make enough soap to last me five years!"

Lies! It's all lies!

Lies, lies…

THAT'S IT! Maybe there are different kinds of lyes!

I race to my computer and call upon the holy internet to see if I'm onto something. And guess what I discover?

Being cheap can get you in trouble. That's what I discover.

Apparently, there are two types of lye. Sodium hydroxide and potassium hydroxide—the latter of which is slightly cheaper. I used potassium hydroxide in my recipes instead of sodium hydroxide, which means I made *a concentrated version of liquid soap instead of solid soap bars?!*

I race back to the kitchen and dig the soap out of the garbage. Don't judge—it was a brand-new plastic liner with nothing else inside but liquid-soap-concentrate goop. I put it all in glass jars and even try some to be sure it works.

Sure as hell does. *Now how about that.*

A week later, I return to the same cosmetic bulk store for a jar of the slightly more expensive sodium hydroxide. I whip together a very basic batch of soap, as per Marie's earlier advice, and wait twelve hours, though I don't know how it's possible.

Lo. And. Behold.

I've just made the most beautiful soap. Ever.

This is where my soap addiction begins.

## DISH SOAP
MAY 22, 2016

I've been using my liquid soap concentrate to clean the dishes. It gets the job done, but I don't like the film on my glassware. Maybe if I spent more time experimenting, I could create something that works for me. I think I'll switch back to my eco dish soap from the bulk store. *Yeah, yeah. Chemicals.*

## LAUNDRY SOAP

When I got into cloth diapering years ago, I discovered Soap Nuts, which are not actually nuts, but berries. After they are harvested, the seed in the middle is removed and the outside is dried. Throw four or five into a little drawstring bag, then put them in the washing machine instead of detergent and they will literally remove the stink from cloth diapers. The best part? You can use the same little bag of soap nuts for four to five washes, in my experience. Additionally, they are compostable. You can even boil them in water to make your own cleaning spray, which is quite effective. I haven't made any since I discovered vinegar and lemons, though. (Someone told me to soak lemon scraps in a jar of vinegar for two weeks. It leaves whatever surface you spray smelling like fresh citrus, and it a helluva mirror cleaner.)

The only downfall I find with soap nuts is that they can make things like towels, cloth pads, and diapers less absorbent over time. Those items then need to be "stripped." Stripping involves bleach and time, and to be honest, I've never had much patience.

In terms of more conventional laundry soap, I started making my own, start to finish, from scratch before my daughter was born, six years ago. The recipe I use most often involves grating a bar of soap, cooking it in water, then mixing it with borax and washing soda, two ingredients which are very easy to find in compostable packaging. It doesn't take very long to make, and each batch makes enough for several months' worth of laundry. It also saves quite a bit of money.

There is some controversy surrounding to the safety of borax, however. But in doing some reading, it seems to be less horrifying than most of the other ingredients in commercial soaps. Additionally, most of the recipes call for using grated Fels-Naptha bars, which I can smell a block away. All that smelly stuff just smells chemical-y in my opinion. Since I've never been able to stand anything perfumed, especially soaps, I've always substituted Fels-Naptha for perfume-free and dye-free bars. Now I can just use my own.

It's amazing to think my homemade detergent passed the Super-Nosey-Husband Test years ago. I swear my ex has the olfactory system of a beagle. He can smell if the laundry has been left rotting the washing machine for two minutes or five. So when I first suggested we try my homemade detergent, before our daughter was born, I knew he was super skeptical.

I didn't let it bother me, however. I proudly announced *I finally made laundry detergent! I can die happy now.* I remember the look on his face as he examined the blob of goop in the bottom of the five-gallon bucket, followed by eyes that said *we'll see about that, you crazy woman.*

Let's just say that I decided right then and there that if this recipe passed the test, I'd use it for life.

I'm still using it, folks.

## AFRICAN BLACK SOAP

I've seen this in every cosmetic supply store: African black soap. I have no idea what it is because it doesn't come in a soap bar but, rather, in loose clumps all packed in a container. So I google it. Hmmm... My eyes skim the words on the screen. I see something about healing the skin, made in West Africa, highest concentration of shea butter... fixes skin problems?

Sold.

So I buy some in bulk.

Now, I typically have great skin. Dry and a few zits around my chin every month, but other than that, I'm very lucky. I joke that my face is probably the dirtiest part of my body because I don't have a regular skincare routine, nor do I wash it often.

For a time, I used coconut oil to remove makeup if my pillowcase didn't do a sufficient job, but then I discovered that baby blankets made of minky material—you know, that super-soft fuzzy stuff—make the best makeup remover ever. You can cut off a piece, run it under water, and use it to remove makeup better than anything because of all those fine fibers. The best part? You can wash it over and over again.

Lately, however, my skin has been dry and full of blackheads, and every time I look in the mirror, I feel gross and way older than I am. One guy in a bar recently mistook me as being nearly ten years older, so I'm really feeling down about myself. Was it the separation? The Québec winter? All the gray hair?

The first time I use African black soap, I have to do a double take. As I walk by the mirror, something catches my eye. It's not that my pants are too tight or my shirt is on backward. Rather, my skin looks really tight.

*Ah. The towel on my head is pulling everything backward, giving me a facelift.*

Except that it's not.

I remove the towel and go in for a closer look. What the…?

My skin hasn't looked this good since I last saw an esthetician two years ago!

I can't believe it. I run back to the bathroom to make sure it doesn't just have to do with lighting. Sure enough, my skin looks tighter. My pores are nearly invisible. How is this possible?

So to celebrate, I throw on some moisturizer and wear an outfit that resembles something Forever 21-ish. You know, shorts above the knees.

## MONTH FIVE RECAP:
MAY 29, 2016

My diet is changing. I'm eating healthier and better, I

think, now that I buy stuff in my own containers. It turns out I also have a passion for unsweetened dried mango and chocolate-covered almonds. Who knew?

My worm bin seems to be doing well. I have to leave the lid off so the compost doesn't turn the inside into a sauna. I didn't realize how much heat composting produces. I dig around from time to time to see if all the worms are still alive. My apartment still smells earthy, in a good way, and not at all moldy or rotten like I worried about. It's making me want to garden, which is impossible in an apartment building like this unless I commit to window gardening. But I just don't have enough light.

# CHAPTER SIX:
## SAFETY RAZORS
### JUNE 9, 2016

I've been doing an awful lot of wondering lately. What's better? Shaving, electrolysis, or laser hair removal? What's the zero-wastiest option, besides doing nothing? I guess it depends on the amount of hair you're looking to remove.

Last year, I received the gift of laser hair removal from a boyfriend. I could have been mad, but instead I chose to look at the situation honestly. Was cuddling with me in the winter akin to rolling around with a giant block of sandpaper?

*Yes.*

Was I ready to spend a bunch of money on long johns when I could just grow a pair myself?

Heck no. *That's what you call ingenuity.*

The problem was that my ingenuity—rather, my laziness—was sort of a sticking point—no pun intended—in my relationship. And so my dearest, darling boyfriend paid for me to laser my legs and bikini.

I struggled with the idea of laser. I don't know much about it. I don't know if it's safe or if it's going to cause some sort of weird cancer down the line. *Is it going to hurt worse than a tattoo? Or childbirth?! How many sessions will it take?*

Turns out it takes hair types like mine around twelve sessions, and it isn't that painful actually, unless the technician forgets to reset the laser and uses the tolerance setting of the previous patient who happens to have no feeling in their body whatsoever. That only happened once, and it smelled like a branding afterward because of all the burnt hair follicles. What is with me and burning hair?

But I can get past that.

What I can't get past, however, is the fact that the middle-aged technician with the weird accent seems to really get a lot of enjoyment out of the bikini portion of the laser session. Once, at the recommendation of a friend, after I mentioned I didn't think the laser removal was doing much, I let the hair on my legs and bikini grow out *one* single day so the technician could get a visual of where the laser was actually working. You know, so she could make sure to hit those visibly stubbly parts with a little more gusto.

The technician took one look and said she'd need to *shave me* before proceeding. *Fine,* I thought. *Maybe she took a clear mental note of all the patches?*

I thought she'd just do the legs, so I put on my laser goggles and pretended I was at some spa down south. I've been shaved before for surgeries; this was going to be a breeze.

But then she shaved the bikini area too. With a little too much enthusiasm, if you ask me.

I didn't move. I just kept staring at the poster of the beach on the wall, repeating *I love myself, I forgive myself,* a technique I learned from said highly enlightened boyfriend, while she sang jovially. It was so awkward; I haven't been back since. And I've had awkward moments on the waxing table in the past, as any woman has.

I guess waxing could be zero waste if you're using honey or sugar wax and cotton strips. But I hate the feeling of having hair ripped out of my body. It's just too much. I like to keep things painless, and the only thing I can think of that comes close is shaving with a razor.

Now stop for a second! Imagine this! Someone like me goes through probably the equivalent of fifty razors per year. I mean, if I cared about shaving all the time, that would be the minimum. Right now, I'm using the razors from Costco, which come with one handle and multiple blades, so it's eco-friendlier. But it's not eco-friendly *enough* for this project.

Think about all that trash! And if every woman is producing this kind of razor trash, that means there are literally *mountains and mountains* of razors—Intuition, Venus, and Quattro—taking up dump space! Everybody I know just throws them in the garbage. I don't know if they're easily recyclable. I doubt it.

So I'm going to try something that scares the living bananas out of me this month. **I'm going to buy a safety razor**—yes, from like the 1900s—and I'm going to try shaving with that. I'm pretty sure I'll cut myself at least ten times and maybe even remove an appendage, but hey, all in the name of *zero waste*, yeah?

So I order my razor from a fancy online company that sells these things in so many different styles and forms that I want to buy three of every option available. But I can't. Not until I know I actually like the sucker. Also, that wouldn't be very zero waste of me.

I buy a standard, inexpensive one with a long handle, something I read that was important in a thread online, with the thought that if I like this so much, I'd eventually save up for the one with a beautiful stone handle. I have no idea how many blades, or even what type, to buy so I settle on the second-cheapest option. One hundred blades for eighteen bucks. Each side can be used for up to four shaves – as in legs, bikini, and underarms – which means each blade can provide a total of eight full shaves. Wait a minute…

Judging by the looks of it, I bought enough blades to last me until retirement and at a price a hell of a lot cheaper than all the razors I've been using. I did fork over a few extra dollars for a metal used-blade container. If I throw the old blades in there, I can put the whole thing in the recycling bin to be melted down at the recyclers. *Or so they say.*

Now, here comes the exciting part.

Shaving.

I'm so nervous I'm going to reenact my first experience, I think I might need a shot of whiskey. If I drink enough, I won't even feel if I cut myself, so that sounds like a good idea.

I was fifteen when I shaved my legs the first time, which by comparison to my peers, was about three years too late. My mom tried to keep me and my sister, Josie, from shaving anything, especially our legs, by telling us what a pain in the butt it was to keep up with.

*Remember, kids, once you start, the hair turns black and gets really thick, like pubes. Then you're burdened with having to shave your pubey legs every day for the rest of your life. Be warned!*

But after a few awkward experiences in junior high that revolved around outdoor gym class, freezing cold weather, shorts, and blonde leg fur which transformed into that tall strip on a dog's back when it senses danger—in my case, only goose bumps—I decided I'd suffered enough embarrassment. My one and only friend even laughed at me.

So, one morning, I finally decided to shave using the razor *all* fifteen-year-olds used back then: their mother's single-blade pink Bic. Or as I like to call it, The Resurfacer. I used lots of soap, just like they said to on the commercials, but I still managed to slice off the front part of one shin like a cheese grater. I can still feel it if I close my eyes.

Please, let this experience be a little better…

I watch a few YouTube tutorials about shaving with a safety razor for the first time. This doesn't look so bad. I just have to follow the rules:

- Don't push down on the razor.
- Let it glide with its own weight.
- Use a good shaving soap; I'm using my own.
- Don't rush. *Great.* I'm always in a rush when I'm shaving. Who isn't?

Here we go…

Sweet Jesus, Mary, and Joseph.

I don't know how, but I didn't cut myself! Not even once! And my legs are so smooth, I'm rubbing them together like a grasshopper. This feels just like the five-blade razors. Should I be so shocked? I'm actually so impressed, I'm considering shaving other parts of my body just to make sure it's not too good to be true. Like my toes. Or maybe my face. Surely I could use a little detailing around the eyebrows.

This is great. I can't believe it.

I just told my ex-mother-in-law about my new safety razor, and she gave me the "been there, done that, way ahead of you, toots" look. Why did society switch to disposables? These are so much classier, so much cooler-looking… and also really difficult to travel with on an airplane?

Great. The world wide interweb is telling me I can't fly with a safety razor in my carry-on. Since I rarely check baggage, it seems I'll have to find another solution. I guess I'll keep my disposable with the changeable heads for flying. I also just discovered blade sharpeners exist, so maybe that's worth a go. I'll use my new safety razor for everything else.

## MONTH SIX UPDATE:
JULY 3, 2016

I'm running a little behind schedule, but that's okay. I've been shaving with my safety razor for a couple of weeks now, and I'm really impressed. I also think I should have forked over more money for the better blades. The one that comes with the razor is the expensive blade which shaves so close and clean it gets you hooked. I took the cheap ones, so I have to use a lot of soap and change them every three shaves. But I don't regret my decision. Yet.

What else. I harvested worm casings (compost) for the very first time last week.

I'm not as psyched about it as I hoped I would be because, as it turns out, I just didn't have enough worms to process all this food! I also made a huge mess.

I have a very tiny balcony, and it was very hot out, so in a moment of sheer genius, I decided the best way to go about collecting worm poop would be to cover my beautiful wood floors with a cheap—there's that word again—tarp and harvest indoors out of the sun and fresh air.

I nearly gagged when I tipped the bin over. Worms poured out, as did a mixture of molding food and newspaper. It wasn't at all as dry as the compost I'd seen in the YouTube videos. It was wet and *blobular*, which is a term I just invented.

And then came the smell of pig shit.

That's exactly what it smelled like! But I didn't let this deter me... too much. I ran into the kitchen where the air was fresh, put on some rubber gloves, and took a deep breath. (I can hold my breath for a very long time thanks to all my years singing powerhouse ballads. One of my nicknames is Horse Lungs.)

I worked in forty-five second intervals for maybe twenty minutes, pausing for air, then pulling worms out of *blobs* of *blobbiness*. I don't know what bothered me more, the worms or the smell. Which is funny, because never once did my bin put off a smell like this when I was feeding it scraps. I guess the layers of newspaper locked it in.

I had a second bin ready with fresh newspaper and scraps for the worms I picked out of the heap, this time with even more holes drilled into the sides for better air intake.

Finally, I finished. I pulled up the corners of the tarp to contain the mess. A few worms managed to wiggle through somehow, but I'd deal with them later. What I needed to do was deal with all this blobby compost.

When I get to the point where I feel overwhelmed, usually to do with the possibility of failing at something— like making proper compost in this instance—I sometimes shut down. So I put the "compost" in the last garbage bag I had left in the house and left it on my balcony.

*I'll let it sit there until I figure out what to do with it.*

If I say I'm going to let something sit, it means I'm never going to deal with it again.

The truth hurts sometimes.

That's the exact point when I started giving up on indoor composting. But there was the new bin I had to deal with.

I decided to give composting another go. Clearly, I didn't drill enough holes in my first bin or have enough worms to process all the food scraps. Hopefully, they had multiplied enough for my second attempt to be successful.

But a week or so into the new bin, I had a new problem.

Fruit flies.

I tried every trick on Pinterest to kill them. I just wasn't doing this indoor composting thing right on any account, and I was really feeling like a failure!

Then, while I was on the phone with my sister complaining about something I can't remember, I noticed there was sawdust on the top rim of the bin.

*That's funny. I didn't drill any holes in the wall above it.*

Then I noticed the sawdust was *moving*.

"Ack! I think I know where the fruit flies are coming from!"

"Yuck, Jaren, what're you going to do?"

"Screw it! I'm throwing it out!"

"Gosh, Jaren. All that hard work."

Pause.

And with that, I destroyed five months of hard work.

And now I feel stupid.
And terrible.
So terrible, I cry.

# CHAPTER SEVEN:
## DECLUTTERING THE CLOSET

**clutter-butter [kluht-er buht-er]**
*n.* a person who finds *any* excuse not to get rid of clutter.
"I would get rid of that outfit, *but* I might wear it one day thirty years
from now." "I know I don't use it, *but* someone gave it to me." "*But*
what if they discontinue that model one day?"
Famous clutter-butters: Anyone from TLC'S *Hoarders*;
the author of this here book.

## JULY 4, 2016 – INDEPENDENCE DAY

I have a clutter problem. It goes back as far as I can remember, and I'm not sure who to blame it on. My grandmother, perhaps, for letting me snoop through her drawers for trinkets and old lipsticks when I was little? My dad, for introducing me to thrift stores? Myself? *Never.*

Maybe the clean genes skipped a generation. That doesn't really make sense, though. My sisters are both so organized.

The last three years of high school, I lived with my father so I could attend the state university for my dance courses. On weekends, we'd make the rounds at the flea shops in town. There were three we used to frequent, but one was my favorite. It was situated in a large warehouse near the local roller skating rink and had, by far, the best selection of vintage clothing.

It's there I discovered I had a talent for finding valuable objects. Sometimes, I'd walk by a section of the market and discover something I just couldn't live without. Usually something I wasn't familiar with, like some vintage kitchen gadget or clothing brand I never heard of. Nine times out of ten, I'd discover the item was way out of my budget.

*Wow, I have expensive taste.*

So I started collecting items I believed would be valuable one day, but that I could afford at that moment.

It didn't take long before my bedroom started to resemble something from *Hoarders*. My dad would ask, genuinely, how it was possible I lived in such a mess.

"Doesn't it make you feel bad? You wouldn't spend so much time looking for things if you had a place for everything."

And then he'd recite the most annoying phrase of my entire childhood, second to the Seven P's: proper prior practice prevents piss-poor performance.

"Remember, Jaren. A place for everything and everything in its place."

It may as well be tattooed on my forearm.

But letting go of stuff was so painful. I became the Queen of a Thousand Excuses. (No, though, for real, I had that nickname the longest.)

*"But DAD! I saw one of these, in only slightly better condition, for like $100!"*

*"Laugh now, Dad. But when you're stuck selling all this stuff after I move out, I'm going to make you rich!"*

*"You're only going to take a 10 percent commission, right, Dad?"*

*"Dad?!"*

My attachment to things changed abruptly one summer, in Los Angeles. I was moving in with my now ex-husband and having survived the entire summer away in Sweden on very little, I felt more motivated than ever to sell all my belongings. This way I could move into his tiny, one-bedroom apartment.

So I held a yard sale.

Quite literally *all* of my belongings sat on the sidewalk across the street from my Studio City apartment for hours, and only one person walked by. I sold him an inversion table for $20.

*What a waste. I may as well give this stuff away.*

After an hour or so, Matt called to say he needed me to pick him up from a friend's house just over the hill. I could be back in thirty minutes and, judging by the look of it, my stuff would still be waiting for me, untouched.

But it wasn't.

When I returned, every single item was gone. I was equal parts horrified and liberated. I didn't know how to feel. All I could think about was how much money I lost not being there to negotiate like the pro that I wasn't.

Eventually, I felt gratitude for the experience. I was free of all those possessions which were, at the time, holding me back from a goal. The Universe understood my problem and did me a solid.

But even though I'm not the clutter-butter I once was that fateful day in Los Angeles, I'm still... messy. I can't, for the life of me, remember to put stuff away. I get in a hurry and habitually say to myself, "I'll put it away when I get back." Then I come home to a mess I don't feel like cleaning up.

Only now can I justify having a little bit of clutter based on a conversation Matt and I had with our family psychologist after we separated. He indirectly told Matt to stop obsessing about how clean the kids' room was because "it's important for a child's development to learn how to manage all the *stuff* they have within their own space." I don't know if he meant during the separation, so they had something in their environment they could control since everything else was clearly out of their control, or if he meant in general.

But I'm an adult. What's my excuse? The one thing I do know is that I am a calmer person when my surroundings are clean and less distracting.

**So this month I'm going to get rid of clutter, starting with my closet!** I'm going to downsize my closet into a micro-wardrobe. Sweet mother of mercy, help me.

## JULY 5, 2016

The big day is here!

Taking some advice from a TED talk given by Marie Kondo, author of *The Lifechanging Magic of Tidying Up*, I decide to find all the clothes in my house and put them in one place.

My bedroom floor.

I pile them by kind: shoes, pants, and tops, and weed out what isn't working for me, according to my indecisive inner critic. This is harder than it's supposed to be, I'm pretty sure. Why am I so attached to something made out of fabric? It's just *stuff*!

I hum and haw and eventually ask myself WWMD? It's kind of like asking "What Would Jesus Do," but instead it's "What Would Mom Do?" (I caught her throwing out silk gowns given to her by a princess in Saudi Arabia after a yard sale once because they didn't fit her. I dug them out of the trash can and still have the black nightgown. You're welcome, silk gown. Sometimes my mother can be so heartless.)

The trick worked brilliantly. I stopped feeling anything toward my material possessions and just started piling stuff into garbage bags for donation. Thirty minutes later, I was finished.

Here's the final tally:

**Shoes:** I went from 24 down to 14 6 pairs of flats, 3 pairs of dance, 3 pairs of boots, 1 pair of heels, 1 pair of sneakers

**Skirts:** I never wear them, so I got rid of the 2 I had

**Dresses:** I went from 4 to 1

**Bras:** 9 down to 5

**T-shirts:** 15 down to 4

**Long-sleeve shirts:** 4 to 1

**Camisoles/tank tops:** 18 down to 8

**Pajamas:** 5 to 3 pairs

**Workout tops:** Stayed the same at 4

**Workout bottoms:** From 5 down to 3

**Bodysuit:** 1 (Why do I still have this?)

**Shorts:** 5 to 4

**Pants:** 11 pairs down to 5

**Vests:** 2 (Stayed the same.)

**Sweaters:** 7 down to 2

**Jackets:** 3 down to 2

**Dress pants:** 2 (Stayed the same.)

**Nice dresses:** 3 down to 1

**Dress shirts:** 11 down to 5

**Pantsuit:** I had no idea I even owned one. I never wear it, so I'm getting rid of it.

**Dress jacket:** 1

**Winter Coats:** 2 (A nice one and a regular Quebec Winter one.)

So, in total, I went from 119 items of clothing down to 61 items and from 24 pairs of shoes down to 14.

Not bad.

What will I do with the clothes I got rid of? Donate them to my basement storage unit until I know for sure this was a good idea.

## THREE WEEKS LATER

This was a great idea! I thought for sure I'd miss

JAREN CERF

everything I got rid of, but that wasn't the case! I did miss a couple of things, like a skirt after all, so I'm glad I put everything in the basement and had access to it *just in case.*

Curiously… I do less laundry now that I have fewer things? How's that possible? I'm actually wearing some items, like the occasional T-shirt, *two days in a row.* I know. I can feel the French blood flowing through my veins. I am wearing deodorant, though.

For some reason, I'm naturally taking better care of the clothes I do have, and I'm not using my pant legs or long-sleeves as napkins anymore. My parents must be so proud reading this.

Another side effect of having fewer clothes is that I have less anxiety. Huh?

For years I used to panic about what to wear for work. I'd try on four different things, scream at the top of my lungs that I have nothing to wear, ugly cry, scramble to get to work on time—always five minutes late, always blamed on traffic—then come home to a huge mess of clean laundry mixed with dirty laundry on the floor, which would just make me more outraged.

This was relieved when my daughter was about the age of one. I discovered, via Pinterest, a clever way to get her dressed without a fight by *picking out her clothes the night before.* I couldn't believe I never tried that trick on myself before. How genius! But I'd still have moments of frustration while choosing my clothes for the next morning.

This capsule wardrobe business, though. It's lifesaving! When all the pieces work together, you're never stuck with *nothing to wear.* It's so brilliant, in fact, it totally cancels out the fact that people see me wearing the same clothes all the time. I don't even care. I could be one of those clever fashionistas who finds thirty ways to make an outfit out of four staples and different colored underwear, but I'm just not trying that hard. Is it because I have a new perspective on life now that I'm cleaning it out from top to bottom? Does this mean I now find fashion frivolous and unimportant?

No.

I love fashion. I love how artistic designers can be. But I don't stress about it in my daily life right now because I feel very comfortable in every single item in my tiny closet. As long as I'm comfortable, I'm happy. As long as I'm happy, I smile more. As long as I smile more, I look brighter and prettier. So can it be deduced, then, that people with capsule wardrobes are better-looking than people with closets the size of J-Lo's? Asking for a friend.

## ZERO-WASTE TRAVELING:
### ATTEMPT NO. TWO

I'm going to Toronto for work meetings for four days, and I'm taking the train. Not because I'm trying to be greener—aren't trains a better option than planes, though, in terms of energy consumption and pollution?—but because I might be involved in a project for ViaRail Canada. So, I'm scoping it out, and I'll give my business partner some feedback on my experience.

I had the option of taking the bus, and I love taking busses because they're cheap and have Wi-Fi so I can work the entire trip. But the train also has Wi-Fi, the trip will be shorter, and, more importantly, there will be train attendants doling out hot coffee and, I hope, alcoholic beverages. I just feel like if you're going to take the train, you'd better drink a scotch or something to go along with the scenery. (By the tone of this book, so far, I think it's fair to assume you think I drink a lot. I average one or glasses of wine per week.)

To prepare for my little trip, I looked back at my previous attempt at traveling zero waste in Moscow and decided to make a few adjustments. I wouldn't be traveling by air or by train internationally, so my baggage wouldn't be screened like it is on airplanes. This meant I wouldn't have to worry about packing little zero-waste snacks for myself. I could pack as many as I please.

So I packed two containers of sesame/rice crackers and one container of dried strawberries and dried papaya chunks. I'm questioning my decision to bring the papaya because it typically gives people—not me because I'm perfect in every way—gas. I'm not sure gas and a train car full of people is a good idea, but I like the taste so much I think I'm willing to try.

I'm also bringing a metal water bottle and a metal coffee mug because if there are two things I can't live without, it's coffee and an empty water bottle. I carry it around "just in case," though by now it's probably just for looks.

I've also made sure to bring along a beeswax-coated fabric swatch aka natural saran wrap—thanks for the DIY, Pinterest—in case someone happens to be making sandwiches or selling unpackaged fruit somewhere.

As far as clothing, I've decided to pack lightly. I've packed one pair of pants, a convertible multi-dress I made, three tops, two jackets, one for the weather, one for looks, undergarments—I prefer *undergarments* to the term *underwear*—one pair of sandals in case it's warm, and one set of gym clothes in case I get a wild hair and decide to change thirty-something years of bad habits. Today, I'm wearing a T-shirt, jeans, and sneakers with a scarf I discovered yesterday while cleaning out the depths of my hallway closet. In my mind, the outfit looked like a Pinterest post, casually cool as though it were only put together in three minutes when in reality it took two hours. In my case, it really did only take three minutes. If I'm going to be on a train for five hours, I had better be comfortable. That's how I plan for life: be comfortable.

It's 11:09 a.m. and I've been on the train for an hour now. The ticket checker passed through the aisles asking to see everyone's tickets, and I couldn't help but feel a little bit smug because I wasn't wasting an entire sheet of paper to print a ticket. *Nope. I have my ticket on my phone.* Oh, I feel so technologically advanced right now.

Hmm. That's something I thought I couldn't live without: printing stuff.

When I was with my ex-husband, I printed stuff every day: graphic designs I was working on, lyrics, notes, pictures, this, that, and the other. I have managed to live without a printer for over a year now without feeling like I've missed much. Anytime I get the urge to print something, I just email it to Matt and have him print it. Or, I order prints from an actual printing company. I feel like it's more economical. They get their inks in bulk. But maybe that's offset by the packaging and shipping. Who knows. The printer I use most of the time is located not far from where I live in Quebec, and the packaging is all recyclable or compostable, except the thin plastic film that holds cards and photos together. I don't know what's better. Maybe I should just get a printer and try not to use it as much as I did before. Am I overanalyzing this?

Back to the train ride. I think I came up with an alternative use for my beeswax "natural saran wrap." I'm using it to keep my laptop from sliding off the little seat tray. Mine is on a slant, and I have to prop it up with my knee, which is really annoying. Also, the service around here is slow. It's been an hour and eighteen minutes, and the train attendant still hasn't reached my seat, 13A, with the coffee yet. I would have had one this morning, but I was in a hurry.

So as not to assume my train trip is poor, I'm going to point out a few things I like about the train. The window curtains, for one. The reclining seats are nice. There is a guy seated behind me who obviously didn't get the memo about wearing headphones when watching a movie. I'd hate to have to repurpose my scarf into a strangling device. Why is the coffee taking so long?!

Well, the slow train attendant totally redeemed herself. I asked for a coffee, and she filled my mug to the very top. That's like three cups! Maybe that was her way of acknowledging my greenness by bringing my own mug?

I was feeling really good about myself for a moment until she showed me the menu. I saw the plastic-wrapped cheese plate and my inner three-year-old freaked out, again. So I've already failed and I'm only one hour and thirty-seven minutes into my journey. Yeesh.

Lucky for me, I'm stubborn. If riding the train is the only time during this trip I can't officially be zero waste, then that's okay. The rest of the time I'll be in restaurants and houses, and I'm pretty good at being zero waste in those environments.

## MONTH SEVEN UPDATE:

July was hugely successful in terms of dealing with clutter, and in terms of traveling zero waste, not counting the train rides. But it was a major failure in the sense that I'm still mourning the loss of my worm bin and I haven't figured out a solution. I feel like I let the world down. And now I'm back to using a metal trash bin in my kitchen. It just feels *wrong* that I'm not composting somehow.

# CHAPTER EIGHT:
## CLOTH PADS AND DIAPERS
### AUGUST 8, 2016

I have dimmed the lights on my screen to type this chapter because at the moment I'm on an airplane—zero-waste travel, take three—and sitting where four people can easily read what I'm typing. I was going to say, "If you're a man, feel free to skip this chapter," but now that I've had a good think, I say to heck with that it. *This should be required reading.* As a matter of fact, I'm turning up the brightness on my screen for ALL TO SEE. HEY, EVERYONE! THIS CHAPTER IS GOING TO BE ABOUT PERIODS AND ZERO-WASTE DIAPERING!

There. I feel freer now.

I was pretty much a late bloomer in every sense, growing up: late to get boobs, late to lose my virginity, late to start my period. Not in that order.

It was like torture. Every day, starting in junior high school, I carried a secret stash of pads around waiting for the big day I would finally start my period. I was terrified I wasn't going to feel it and would accidentally bleed all over the place, so I constantly did what every self-conscious teenager awaiting her period does: I tripled-checked my seat and wore layers. My nickname for the longest time was Two Shirts—Horse Lungs, Queen of a Thousand

Excuses, Two Shirts, pick your favorite. Sure, I loved layers, but it wasn't just because I was more prude than the Mormons in my community. I knew if I started my period and bled through my jeans—yes, it's as horrible as it sounds—at least I could tie the extra-long-sleeve shirt around my waist to hide the evidence long enough to reach the nurses office. There, I could call my family in shame and ask to be homeschooled until graduation.

Finally, the big day came. I didn't know what to feel. Luckily, it happened while I was at home and not at school, but I freaked out anyway and decided not to say anything. I remember very vividly sitting on the La-Z-Boy sofa chair when my mom walked into the living room and asked what I was doing using pads. She'd found evidence in the bathroom garbage. Being cheeky, I took a line from one of my favorite books, *Daisy Fay and the Miracle Man* by Fannie Flagg, and said, "Well, I'm not using them to dust hard-to-reach places."

She didn't laugh. *Well, that backfired.*

And when I thought things couldn't get even more awkward, word got round to my dad that his firstborn had finally *become a woman.* So to celebrate my "transition," he surprised me with a dozen red carnations.

I. Was. So. Embarrassed.

Looking back, I think it was very sweet. And you better believe I'm going to throw my daughter a period party like they do in that one commercial on YouTube. Though, hopefully not in the next hundred or so years.

But like most teenagers in my community, I was aware of only two ways to deal with a period: a pad or a tampon. Pads were gross because they were very thick back then, and the sound of the wrapper ripping open in the bathroom stall echoed so loud, it seemed to announce to the entire school that it was that time of the month. Tampons seemed like a better idea, but then there was the problem of TSS, or toxic shock syndrome, if you left them in too long.

*Great… I can die of poisoning or embarrassment. Which is worse?*

There had to be other options. My mom told me about sponges and the "cup," but those were seriously old-school. No way was I going to try them.

Years went by and when I became pregnant with my firstborn, I got the itch to try upstaging Martha Stewart. I wanted to sew and make everything by hand. Cloth diapers seemed interesting and fun because you could choose whatever too-cute-for-words fabric you wanted to adorn your child's bottom. In one of the comment threads, however, one reader posted, "Attention, ladies: If you're really as concerned about the environment and your babies' butts as you say you are, then consider using cloth pads when you menstruate."

I hate that word, menstruate. Mostly, I think, because it has the word "men" in it. And when I menstruate I generally get short with men. *Period.*

The idea of using cloth pads seemed super disgusting. What the hell was I supposed to do with them after eight hours of use?!

*Wash them.*

Yeah, but how?

*Well, you could get a dark, non-see-through container and fill it with clean water. Once you're finished with a pad, you could leave it in the dark container, in an inconspicuous place, until it's time to wash.*

ARE YOU KIDDING ME?! No way!

So I ordered one dozen cloth pads from some mom on Etsy because, once again, curiosity got the better of me. Then I set out to find a dark, inconspicuous container I could hide under my sink.

Here's the thing about using cloth pads. This is going to make me sound a little out-there, though I think we have already established that I am, but the first time I used them was the first time I didn't have debilitating cramps.

Which made me think.

A lot.

I won't go into detail, but suffice it to say, I'd gone to the hospital a couple of times before because of the intensity of the pain. It was like labor, and I can say that because I gave birth twice without pain meds. Not that I'm trying to rub it in. I'm just saying that's how intense—sort of an understatement—the pain was.

I began doing some research online as to why this might be the case.

According to a few online theories, the reason some cramps went away most likely had to do with the fact that there weren't chemicals from the bleached tampons or pads in or near the body. Since it was on the internet, *I knew it was true*. So I switched.

My pain was more manageable, sure, but I also liked the feeling of cloth against my body much better than plastic. There was the issue of cleaning them, but since I was already dealing with diaper changes, I figured *how can I be grossed out with myself if I'm not grossed out by my kids?* So I started to accept the new routine: dirty pads in the dark container under the sink, water changed once a day, machine washed… That's how I did it and I didn't have any problems. And, I felt more connected to myself. I loved myself for *going through all that trouble.*

For this project, however, I wanted to get out of my comfort zone. I needed to experiment with other kinds of feminine products. I wasn't interested in using a sponge or cloth tampons, so instead, I bought a couple of different kinds of cups. The things that attracted me to their use were A) you could wear them longer and B) they really didn't produce much waste.

I started with the Diva Cup. Getting the fit just right so there weren't leaks was a project and a half the first time. So I put it aside for several months because I felt overwhelmed. Eventually, a girlfriend ranted and raved about the Diva Cup, and when I told her my problem, she said "Why didn't you ask me about it?! They are a little weird at first, but once you get the right fit, they're a dream!" So I tried it again, and loved it, as long as I was at home when it was time to change.

Here's the deal with menstrual cups. You're essentially inserting a silicone cup in your body, which catches all the flow so when you remove it, you have to dump the contents in the toilet. Then, you have to rinse it before putting it back in. That's the sanitary thing to do. But it's hard to do when you're on the go. Luckily, I found a solution! Remember that empty water bottle I used to carry around for looks? Well, now I keep it full of water! I can literally rinse the cup in a bathroom stall wherever I am.

But just when I though the Diva Cup was my answer to zero-waste periods, I discovered an even better solution. The cup with a draining device at the end.

Think it sounds completely off-the-wall disgusting? Don't knock it, yet. The idea behind this cup is that you can leave it in for twelve hours at a time and pinch the end to drain it without having to remove it. This has two benefits: convenience and less bacteria from the removal and subsequent reinsertion. (That's also a terrible word—*reinsertion*.)

The only downfall of this second cup, in my opinion, is that depending on the woman's build, it might be too long for her vaginal canal, which sort of causes a pinching sensation. But most come in a couple of different lengths now, so when in doubt, go shorter. That's my advice.

Oh! I did forget to mention one thing. How does one travel zero waste when they're expecting a visit from Aunt Flo? If I'm going out for the day, I carry a "wet bag." Wherever you find wet bags for baby stuff, you'll find wet bags for cloth pads. Basically, it's like a little plastified cloth pouch. I use a plastic-lined pencil pouch myself. In one side, I keep clean pads, and in the other, I keep the dirty ones folded over onto themselves so you don't see anything you don't want to see. The pouch fits easily in a purse, not that I carry one. (If you see me carrying one, you'll know it's that time of the month.)

I don't feel comfortable traveling by plane with cloth pads, however. I just feel like if a TSA member came across them in my bag, clean or not, I'd miss my flight over an embarrassing interrogation and end up on the news with some god-awful headline like, "Zero-Waste Advocate Subjects TSA Officials to Used Sanitary Napkins." *Imagine.* The movement would die in an instant.

So I'll stick with the cup and perhaps keep a pack of regular pads around for instances like that.

## CLOTH DIAPERS

Remember I mentioned I got a little *crafty* during my pregnancies? Both times I must have sewn enough cloth diapers to cover a village full of baby bottoms. I made so many, I had to sell a box full before my son was born, just so I could make room for the new designs I wanted to try *after* he was born. I think there were seventy-something in total. They were all different types and styles because I learned that babies, even though they're all small when they come out of the oven, have different body types. The diapers I thought would work on my daughter simply didn't fit my son. They leaked.

I tried a different pattern but got bored with how they looked. So I made even more by experimenting and modifying an existing pattern until I found the perfect fit. But by then, I'd grown so sick of sewing cloth diapers, I didn't want to make more.

So I purchased some online. (I'm exhausted just typing this.)

I had a love-hate relationship with cloth diapering. I

loved that they breathed. I loved that my kids rarely ever got diaper rashes. I loved that they were comfortable and that I could make them out of the cutest fabric in the world. But I hated the smell of two-day old diapers going into the washing machine—poop-free because you have to dump/scrape it into the toilet, but smelling just the same. *How the hell do they do it in the underdeveloped world?!*

When my daughter was five weeks old, I discovered "elimination communication." The idea is that when we are born, we instinctively know not to pee or poop in our clothes. That's why babies always seem to pee the minute you take *off* their diaper. So, to keep your child free of diapers, you place them over a baby potty and give them sound cues, like "psssss" for number one, or blowing raspberries for number two. Believe it or not, it works. From the time my daughter was a six-week-old, until the age of nine months, we used elimination communication as often as possible. Only at night would we put her in cloth diapers. She became the show poodle among our friends and family as they stared in disbelief that I could cue her to pee and poop on command. Poor child.

That all ended when we moved to Montreal, however. Since we were traveling for two months during the move, we didn't want the stress of cloth diapering and cueing on the road. But once we settled in, we continued the cloth diapering, gradually reverting to disposables after my son was born. Because laziness, duh. Ask any second-time mom.

So I've decided to dig out the ol' cloth diapers for my son, since he still needs them at night. Maybe feeling the wetness will help him train out of them sooner.

I have used so many different types of cloth diapers, but I always revert back to the trifold, used as an insert, with an adjustable PUL outer shell. Clothers will know exactly what I'm talking about. Now I just have to figure out how I'm going to take care of this between washings in an apartment building with no working washer/dryers. I'll only be able to do laundry once per week, so I need to get creative. If it's one thing I detest, it's the smell of stinky pee diapers.

## AUGUST 28, 2016

It's been a week. Well, four days that my kids are actually with me. I have two gDiaper covers, two adjustable PUL covers, and tons of liners. I'm *covered*.

In the morning, my son removes his diaper and puts it in the bathtub. I immediately rinse it out with hot water and wring it out as much as I can. Then I throw it in the laundry pile and wash my hands twice. Because eww! (I have to make my kids breakfast, my daughter's lunch, and my coffee, and I don't want any of it smelling like toddler pee.)

As long as I rinse the cloth inserts out well, they don't seem to smell as bad as I remember. I mean, it's only been a year and a half that I stopped using them so regularly. Maybe my mom brain is playing tricks on me, but this seems easier than I thought it would be.

The hardest part about cloth diapering, in the beginning, is the *idea* of it, in my opinion. I always imagined it would be this terribly difficult task, as so many people warned me about. So I made great efforts to streamline the whole process for myself so I would stick with it, because like any first-time mom, I wanted to do everything *right*. I wanted to protect my child from all the havoc man was wreaking on Mother Earth with all its pesticides, plastic, and carcinogens. Nothing was going to touch my baby.

Then I had my son. I was a little more relaxed by the time he came around. Heaven forbid I have a third—it'll have to diaper itself.

I guess, as it is with trying anything new, acceptance is the key to success. And you can't accept something without first being open to it. So with something as silly as cloth diapering, simply accepting the fact that it's okay for me to do it my own way, even though the majority of people do it differently, makes it easier for me to stick with. The same applies to every experience I've had up to this point in my zero-waste journey. It's not always easy, but then life isn't always easy. And there's something to be said about being open and flexible to new ideas. With flexibility comes adaptability, and with adaptability comes a great sense of freedom, because then you're never a victim of circumstance. At least for very long. Now that's some deep shit.

## MONTH EIGHT RECAP:

Well, since I got rid of disposable tampons and pads, I figured I may as well get rid of Kleenex and paper towels too. To be honest, I've been using cloth rags in place of paper towels for a very long time thanks to a guerilla marketing campaign which ended in boxes of leftover hockey towels. But I find that paper towels are impossible to replace when it comes to making bacon. *How in the hell are you supposed to absorb the grease?* I'm not going to use the rags, *obviously*. I don't want to start a dryer fire, but this really bothers me. I need to find a solution.

Kleenex isn't missed. I use toilet paper or little cloth Kleenexes I whipped up on the sewing machine. My mother-in-law has horrific memories, as a child, of being forced to clean dirty hankies, so I'll reserve them for non-sick use. I can't imagine cleaning flu boogers out of cloth by hand.

As for the safety razor, I'm still using it and still loving it. Oh, and I can't stop making soaps. I've made ten different types so far.

JAREN CERF

# CHAPTER NINE:
## MELTDOWN

"C'MON, MOM...GET OUT OF BED!"

AUGUST 8, 2016

I've been debating for several weeks now whether or not I should write down what I'm going to write down. Since this zero-waste experiment is part of what pulled me out of the fire, so to speak, I've decided to go ahead.

This chapter has to do with depression and mental disorders. Just a heads-up.

After having become 90 percent zero waste, according to my own calculations, life happened. My plans were suddenly interrupted—HOW DARE YOU, LIFE!— by the loss of a business I had invested nine months of my life building. But it was more than that. I'd also grown tired of the music industry I had spent the previous twelve years of my life slaving away for in hopes I could make a decent living. A single conversation with a well-respected individual in the electronic dance music industry convinced me it was time to end my career.

For months prior to the dissolution, my days and nights, until the wee, wee hours, were spent working. I rarely socialized. The only people I interacted with regularly were my children. I ate only when I remembered to—a light meal and a few snacks usually—but mostly I survived on coffee because I was too focused on my big plans to make my projects work.

My ex-husband use to complain about my ability to block him out when I was working. I'd be so focused on whatever I was working on, I wouldn't hear him walk into the room and ask me a question. He'd get tired of trying to get my attention and leave. This problem was one of a few which led to our separation.

I had a problem, he said.

"Yeah, you're my problem. What are you talking about?!" I'd joke.

I was in complete denial. But after all of this, I started to think maybe there really was something wrong with me.

Being the serial solution finder I am, I told myself I would look into getting a psychiatric evaluation. I needed answers.

But I was terrified.

What was I going to do? What if there *was* something wrong with me? What if I had to change my entire way of life? *HUH?!* WHO AM I IF NOT A STRUGGLING ARTIST?!!

Then suddenly, my grandmother's favorite saying magically popped into my head.

"If you want to make God laugh, tell her your plans." *Not now, Grandma!*

So I pushed off the evaluation.

I quit everything.

I quit writing this book.

I went numb.

Then I cried.

I screamed at the neighborhood librarian for making me walk *into* the library to return my books, because she locked the outside book drop during daytime hours. I yelled at the father of a child who attended the same day care for snapping at someone else's child. To the point I wanted to punch him.

I yelled at my kids.

I lost two close friends.

And then I called my ex-father-in-law to come over one morning and take the kids so I could go seek help, because I was afraid I was going to want to do something silly... like... check out.

*You know what's really zero waste? Me not being around to produce it. There. I said it.*

I didn't tell anyone about the intensity of my feelings. I was raised to be an independent person. The thought of being reliant, or dependent on someone else for my happiness, made me feel like a failure at life. Feeling like this in front of my children made the pain even worse. And if I couldn't control my feelings, if I couldn't get myself out of this mess, then was I really...

*Eek! Jaren, stop thinking those things! Go get help, now!*

The minute my father-in-law took the kids, I jumped in my car and drove to the local counseling center. I tried to play down my feelings to the intake nurse, *because I didn't want to be dramatic,* but she saw right through me. (I firmly believe crying to be a wonderful release and I encourage it in others. Just not myself, for some reason.) And when the counselor walked in, the flood gates opened.

With the most comforting, motherly-but-not-smotherly voice, she validated my pain, asked a lot of questions, and gave me a safe place to ugly cry out of my nose. (At this point I was *not* using reusable hankies, thankfully, because I would have used the equivalent of three beach towels and who wants to clean that mess.)

I didn't want someone to solve my problems for me. I just needed someone to listen, shake their head, and say "I understand. That really sucks. How can I help?" Because, the thing is, when shit hits the fan, I don't necessarily want someone to take over and clean up my mess. I want to do that myself so I can maintain some sense of control in my life. But, I need to be asked *"How can I help?"* like it's an option, you know? *I'll always say it's okay, I've got this.* I just need the intention to get me through. (My dad is the only man I know who understands this concept. He called every day, sometimes twice a day after the fallout, but there's only so much you can do when you live two thousand miles away.)

Eventually, I brought up the possibility of having ADHD. The first boyfriend I had, after the separation, asked in a loving and gentle way if I'd ever been diagnosed with ADHD. I laughed and almost punched him.

*That shit was made up by the pharmaceutical companies to sell drugs, are you kidding?!*

But he insisted. His friend had been diagnosed in his fifties and learned tools to help him cope. We had similar traits.

I did hours of research. When I came across *hyper-focus,* I broke down in tears. My entire childhood suddenly made sense! I wasn't a crazy black sheep after all! Having ADHD didn't mean you were necessarily fidgety all the time, because I certainly wasn't. But I *could* work on a project for twelve hours straight without eating, because I did it regularly. I couldn't stick to *just being* a songwriter. Or being a recording artist. Not when I could also be a dancer, choreographer, director, screenwriter, book writer, poet, painter, artist… Was this going to be the rest of my life? I'd already failed several business endeavors.

So the counselor wrote me a note for a referral so I could finally have that psychiatric evaluation. And both the psychiatrist and the third-year student both came to an agreement.

I had moderately-severe to severe ADHD. And everything that goes with it.

Drugs were an option, but probably not the most effective one, for my particular case. What I needed was emotional support. Someone to be accountable to, kind of like a drill sergeant. *Hell, I knew that.*

So in one very long appointment, my life had been validated. She said I'd probably go through a period of mourning, and that was okay. Months later I still sometimes have trouble reconciling it.

Six months have passed. In that time, I found myself repeating "I love myself and I forgive myself" tens of times per day and consciously reminding myself to let go, which I found difficult. An article in a music magazine had come out right after my business dissolved, taking a negative tone about all my creative endeavors. A DJ I had worked with for years berated me in a meeting when I pitched a multimedia project in an attempt to put food on the table. He said, as he did many years prior, that *if I could just focus on one skill*, like songwriting or being a recording artist, maybe I wouldn't be so angry that I never made it. I was getting hit right and left.

Eventually, I ran out of tears and the only place to go was up.

There's a quote by Carrie Fisher about losing your mind. Something to the effect of when you finally lose it, you're free to rebuild and start over. That's when I realized I wasn't breaking down, after all.

I was breaking through.

And maybe my having ADHD was a blessing in disguise.

I eventually found a job through the help of a friend and decided I was going to quit writing music and books altogether so I could focus on rebuilding my life. The Universe had other plans, however, and would often remind me by dangling carrots in front of my face with music industry written all over them. But I wasn't stupid. I could ignore them if I could find a distraction.

So I found one.

*** Feel free to warm up the muscles in your face – you're going to be rolling your eyes a lot at this next part.

I started dating my boss.

I know. I sometimes feel like a cat. Either stupidity or curiosity gets the better of me, I'm still not sure which. Doesn't matter. I started what felt like a very loving and helpful relationship in a time when I was really feeling down and needed a positive distraction; he owns a flower shop, and it's difficult to be sad around bright-colored flowers. It was wonderful. Also, the job allowed me to focus on the non-music-industry-related storytelling I so loved: film, blog posts, conducting interviews, etc. Suffice it to say, I didn't write any of this down in my five-year life projection last year.

**Now, despite all this change, one thing always remained: my new habit of consuming less.** And in all actuality, it was the one area of my life where I did maintain some sense of control. I regressed a bit, maybe dropping into the 60 percent range, but I was still much better off than when I started this whole project. Shopping for products without packaging was still doable. I kept reusable bags in my car. I tried only to buy what I needed and spent whatever money I managed to hold on to for experiences, like trips to the children's museum and trade shows, which are horrible places to go if you're not in the mood to reject everyone's offer for business cards and stupid flyers. I even tried to convince my boss to get his eco-certification and start composting all his flower waste.

The biggest challenge about boyfriend/boss—or boyfross, as I'll call him—was that our living styles were fundamentally quite different. Having just gone through a painful divorce a few years earlier, he was forced to sell his big, beautiful, newly renovated house for a much smaller apartment, and he wasn't exactly excited about the transition. I felt his pain. When my ex and I split, I moved across the street to a one-bedroom apartment with the two kids. I wasn't inviting friends over for dinner parties, if you know what I mean. We had that in common, it seemed.

Still, my relationship with boyfross was forcing me to challenge my eco-mentality. Since our relationship was new, I felt guilty divulging exactly how eco-conscious I had become. *All the shampoo bottles in his bathroom are driving me nuts. All those chemicals… is any of this even getting recycled?* So I started slowly, and with the help of his super-cool daughters.

Christmas was just around the corner, boyfross and I had only been dating a couple of months, and I wanted to make a good impression on his daughters. I needed to come up with Christmas gifts that would score me cool points without breaking the bank, but while also being eco-friendly. Bath bombs and sugar scrubs! Preteens would enjoy this kind of activity, right? So I gathered all the ingredients we'd need and spent one evening after dinner leading them through the entire experience, start to finish.

While we were mixing together our ingredients, I told them a bit about Marie Rayma's book and about how she was grossed out by all the chemicals in commercial cosmetics. The youngest daughter made a face.

"Chemicals?! That's gross!"

*Yes! One down, one to go.*

"Yeah," I said. "But isn't fun that you can make your own bath bombs now?"

"Jaren, how did you learn to do this!" she demanded.

"In another life, I started writing a book about becoming zero waste." Boyfross was in the other room, and I was speaking loud enough that he could hear. I'd test him later.

"What? What is zero waste?"

Cue the soapbox, lights, camera, and... action! "I thought you'd never ask. It's where you try to reduce your waste to zero. That means no taking out the garbage. Can you imagine?"

"What?! What do you mean?"

"Well, for example, you know when you brush your teeth? You throw the toothbrush out after it gets old, right? So if you're zero waste, you might use a compostable one instead so you aren't creating any waste. I have some with me—wanna try?" *Yes, I keep new, compostable toothbrushes on me to give away. If that makes me a weirdo, so be it.*

This kid is a trooper, let me tell you. I had her brushing with bamboo in thirty seconds flat. She was so excited, she FaceTimed her mom to show-and-tell her the news. *Mom wasn't thrilled.*

Eventually, boyfross asked me what was the point. *Toothbrushes don't take up much space in the dump*, he said. I questioned whether I liked him enough to continue our relationship after that comment, but decided if I could convert his daughters, perhaps we could convert him together. Three guilt trips are better than one. As it was, his oldest daughter was complaining about trips to the dollar store.

"Dad! Did you know everything there is made by kids in China? And it's overloading our landfills!"

Okay, maybe that was a hasty generalization, but he felt bad about it. None of this zero-waste stuff was on his radar—and then when it was, via me, it came across as overwhelming. So as not to discourage him, I pointed out that he was already pretty good in terms of waste production.

"Look," I said. "Don't feel bad. You only produce one small can of garbage per week. That's already an improvement over most people I know."

It was true. But I gave him a bamboo toothbrush anyway.

Weeks passed, and soon I was spending half my time at boyfross's place. I felt guilty the first ten times I used his Nespresso machine, and only assuaged the guilt a bit by reading about the recycling program on the back of the Nespresso pod collection bag they give out with the purchase of more pods. That was enough justification for me to continue having two or three coffees per day. Besides, I told myself, I'm not buying individually wrapped snack packs or *something wasteful like that.*

But, in all the travel back and forth, I had started easing back into convenience packaged goods. It's just easy to do when your mind is juggling so many places and people at once. I understand why tired parents just want convenience, but somehow all my prior zero-waste work had seeped into my bones and changed my wiring. All this convenience was starting to affect my conscience.

And then a new problem appeared. I started resenting my tiny apartment.

Compare and despair is back with a vengeance.

Last night, after a long phone conversation with boyfross, I felt inspired to watch some Kirsten Dirksen tiny-home videos on YouTube. Maybe all the clever architecture and design would inspire me to feel better about my tiny apartment. *What if you treated your apartment like a tiny home?* boyfross inquired.

I wasn't resisting the idea. I'd do anything to feel better about my living situation. So I marathon-ed about two hours' worth of tiny-home videos. Which brought me back to zero waste. And minimalism.

I need to get rid of all the extra stuff in my apartment *holding me down!*
Yes. That sounds like a great idea.

I guess that means I'm back now.
That feels wonderful to write, I've got to admit.

# CHAPTER TEN:
## SAYING 'NO' TO CLUTTER
### MARCH 5, 2017

Gosh. Maybe I'm biting off more than I can chew.

After going back and rereading these chapters, I realize if I ever want to reach 100 percent zero waste—in my house, I mean—I'm going to have to get more strict about saying "no" to trash. This is difficult for me. I don't like telling people no. I never want to hurt my friends' feelings when they give me something wrapped in tons of packaging, because I'm so overcome with appreciation that they thought to give me a gift in the first place. The last thing I want to do is tell them, *hey, do you mind not wrapping gifts you want to give me? Or better yet, don't give me anything because I think I want to become a minimalist.*

This is also why I have a tough time getting rid of stuff. What can I say; I'm sentimental.

But my refusal to say no is what got me into this mess in the first place.

Why is it so hard to refuse something?! Isn't there a way to do it politely?

Sure! But that doesn't guarantee the refuse-ee doesn't get pissed off or upset by your refusal, polite as it may be.

And let's be honest, there are some people I just don't feel like pissing off. Namely my kids' teachers, anyone serving my food, or anyone working for the city. Because *duh*.

In month three, I did a little experiment at my local grocery store. I tried to convince the lady behind the deli counter to use my containers for sliced meats. She wasn't having it, even though I asked first, very politely. So I went back through ZeeDub's materials and came across a video of how she addresses this topic. The key to successfully convincing someone to use your container, apparently, is to hand it to the person who is going to fill it, while pretending to look busy figuring out which products you might want to put in it. If they see you are clearly distracted by the thought of what to purchase, they're less likely to interrupt your transaction and do what you ask.

Turns out she was right. This worked a handful of times, though not at the same place I tried before. I was too shy to ask again because I thought the lady at the counter would recognize me. Small businesses tend to want to keep your business and seem willing and mostly enthusiastic when you're trying to be zero waste. At least they do here in Montreal.

But how do you politely refuse stuff you don't want in your home? I found a few easy ways to say no to other people's containers over the past year. These worked best for me:

· *May I leave this here? I don't have a trash can at home. Thanks so much!*

· *It's okay, let's use this bag (container) instead. I'm doing the zero-waste thing for a year. It's for work. (People find this irresistible and will probably ask you loads of questions. Or, they'll totally ignore you.)*

· *Is it okay if I take a picture of that instead of taking it home? (For important papers)*

There's still room for improvement, but I think that's a

good start. At least until I find my groove again. Until then, I need to reboot my zero-waste life by getting rid of clutter. This time, not just in my closet.

We have this brilliant app here in Canada—maybe it's worldwide, I don't know—called Varagesale, as in virtual garage sale. You take a picture of what you have to sell and people can contact you. It's like craigslist but easier to use and verified through Facebook. It comes in especially handy when you want to get rid of something very quickly. Just last night, I posted a desk to give away, and it was out of my apartment this afternoon.

This is going to be a really handy app for this project. The goal will be to get rid of everything I don't use regularly. If it's been sitting in my closet for a year and I haven't used it, I need to sell it, donate it, or store it in the basement if I don't have the balls to do either of the first two. Clothing, kitchenware, bedding included.

It's amazing how easily stuff just sneaks into my house. Much less in the kitchen now that I've returned to buying food in my own containers. But the kids' room is a little crazy, even though we've been trying to implement the *one in, one out* rule for a couple of years now. (For every new item my kids get, they need to give up an old one they no longer use.) They're old enough that they understand the concept, but sometimes it's easier for the cleaning fairy to take care of this while they're away at school. Now before you get all judgy, let me say my kids have never asked for something the cleaning fairy got rid of. I know my kids, and I know what they don't play with. So far, at least.

So, technically, I started this month's "JUST SAY NO TO CLUTTER" challenge last night when I cleaned out my desk. I put all the office supplies together, all my papers together, and went to town. It took me four hours, but I now have two bags full of perfectly usable office supplies I either don't use, or haven't used, in the past two years. I also found other things from my living room, like a rug that doesn't fit my style anymore.

Is it weird I feel lighter?

My living room is quite open now that I don't have a giant desk taking up half the room. Instead, I installed wall-mounted shelving, zero waste apart from the small barcode stickers on the shelves. I took a cue from a Pinterest post and created an urban jungle to make my writing corner feel more lively, and boy, don't I love it. I have three real plants on my shelf/desk and two fake ones, and darnit does it ever look beautiful. It's clean and organized, and the best part is I am now getting the hang of "multipurpose" upcycling, which I will explain in a different chapter.

I'm also just about ready to go through my closet a second time to see where I'm at. I have accumulated a few items since my last purge thanks to a birthday, Christmas, generous friends, and my new obsession with CrossFit. (I took my psychiatrist's advice about the whole drill sergeant thing literally, and it's made a difference. *Also, I swear I'm stronger when I wear nice workout leggings.*)

Finally, I will be reorganizing my kitchen and bedroom, keeping my new minimalist-inspired tiny-home vision in mind. Can't be that hard…

I'm staring at a stack of clothes and toys on my living room floor. I've been cleaning for a couple of hours now, and something just occurred to me. Back in the days, before we had immediate access to goods, we took better care of the items we *did* have because that's all that was available to us. We couldn't just throw away a shirt because we didn't like how the color was one shade off from the current "hot" color. We probably couldn't afford too many shirts to begin with, so we took better care of the ones we had. I wonder if we deepened our understanding and appreciation of them, like meditation.

Everything is so disposable in our society, now. Don't like that styled pant? *Throw it out.* Don't like that cell phone? *Get a new one.* I rarely hang on to a piece of clothing for more than a couple of years. Shoes are a little easier, but it's just so easy to be dissatisfied with material objects and to replace them.

When I was a teenager, my ballet teacher, who acted as a second mom in a way, used to carry in her car an old Motorola cell phone, the black flip phone version. You remember. It was outdated, even then, but she wasn't in a hurry to replace it, I suppose, because it fulfilled the functions she required at the time. That was the first time I ever thought about this concept. I appreciated the fact that she held on to it as long as she did. Just like I appreciated my mom for having the same Honda Civic for twenty years without upgrading. She took such good care of it, and in turn, it took wonderful care of us. I wonder if she ever felt pressured to get something newer.

I find myself thinking about this a lot, lately. Especially as it relates to my car, a Mazda 5. It has all the functionality of a minivan, but the maneuverability of a car, so parking in Montreal isn't such a pain. The minute this model entered the marketplace, I knew I wanted one. Then, seven years later, I was a proud owner and I've been driving one since. (Dear Mazda, have your people call my people.)

Would I feel comfortable taking this minivan to Vale, Colorado, and parking it among the Lamborghinis? Yes, actually. I would. I can finally appreciate nice cars. For years, I thought they were a waste of resources. But I can also appreciate the value of practicality without having to *compare and despair.* This is something I've had to practice.

So, with that in mind, I'm making a mental note of the items in my house I've had for longer than five whole years—boy, that doesn't sound like a lot when I read it out loud. Not a tremendous amount: a handmade Hopi bowl, vintage display case and antique refrigerator from my late grandmother, my first guitar, an antique Native American necklace, mementos of my children's births, letters my mother wrote to me as a child… That's pretty much anything I'd want to take with me if my house ever caught fire. Those are the material possessions that matter most. There are a few pieces of art I hope I'll hang on to, like paintings from my ex-mother-in-law, and my sketches of nude models from an art class we take together.

The common thread? Art. That seems to be what I value. The rest is wonderful and functional, but not necessary in terms of making me happy. If I can hold on to this notion, perhaps getting rid of the excess will be easier?

## MARCH 19, 2017

Today, I'm piling all the stuff which fits in the *I know I don't need this* category, in my living room. I'll go through, take pictures of the items I can sell for more than ten dollars per item, and donate the rest, staring with the entryway.

## ENTRYWAY

When I first arrived in Montreal, I thought the streets in the Plateau, a neighborhood in Montreal, were reminiscent of *Sesame Street,* with their sometimes winding, sometimes vertical stairways. The apartments are very long, usually consisting of many rooms off one long, main hallway. In my case, the main door opens smack dab in the middle of the hallway, so you either must go left, toward the kitchen, or right, toward the living room. If you go straight, you'll hit the mess of winter coats and snow boots piled on the floor. This makes opening my door a pain in the butt most of the time.

I thought I fixed my problem when I set-up a stand-alone wardrobe, but as my children get older, their winter clothes get bigger and take up more space. So to solve the inevitable morning doorway jam, I decided to get rid of it entirely. From now on, extra coats will hang in the closet next door, like they do in normal people's houses. I just have to clean it out first to make room. Right now, it's a holding cell for all the crap I can't find a home for. And there's lot of crap.

## ENTRYWAY CLOSET

We all have a junk drawer in our house. Usually, it's located in a desk or a dresser somewhere. Mine happens to be a closet. Inside, you'll find a mishmash of clothes, tool kits, a giant drawer organizer with all sorts of crap inside, craft kits, soap-making supplies—locked up high and out of the reach of small children—storage shelves I may put up one day, and a food dehydrator. In case I become a raw vegan or something. You just never know with these experiments.

So, I take everything out and start putting it in the donate or recycling pile.

*Minimalist tiny home, minimalist tiny home, minimalist tiny home...*

Wow.

Out of that tiny closet, I managed to get rid of three big bags of stuff I don't use. I'm getting the hang of this.

## LIVING ROOM

Now that my hallway closet and entryway are cleaned, I get going on the living room. Since I already cleaned my office area and gave away that huge desk, the focus is more on transforming what little furniture I do have into something which will work for me long term.

Since I share a one-bedroom apartment with my two kids, my big double bed has been in the living room. Two twin beds make up the kids' room, which is quite spacious.

For a while, this worked, but there's just something about not having a designated sleeping area that makes me feel inadequate. So I've decided to move my big bed into the kids' bedroom and share the room with them for a while. You know, see how it goes while they're still little. For years I wanted a Murphy bed so I could cleverly disguise my sleeping space, but I think by now we all know that would be a waste of money because I'd leave it out all the time, completely defeating the purpose.

So I move my bed into the bedroom and my daughter's twin bed into the living room. With pillows against the wall, it looks just like a nice sofa. I can sleep there no problem if this whole experiment blows up in my face. And at least my living room now looks like a proper living room/office.

After learning about furniture-free living—that's another experiment I'll eventually write about—I decide to convert my dresser to a standing desk. It's brilliant and the drawers are home to all my office gear and paperwork. Dressers make way better storage units than desks. The added benefit is that I am getting a lot more physical activity in during my days. The first two days took a bit of getting used to. As long as my back wasn't hurting, I'd continue standing, occasionally moving around or doing a few squats between work assignments. I think my posture has improved, and I might actually be taller. (Update: I measured myself. Turns out I shrunk three-quarters of an inch since I had my kids. But perhaps I shrunk a full inch and gained a quarter-inch since I started standing at my desk? I guess we'll never know.)

So now I'm down to seven pieces of furniture in my living room. My dresser/desk, my sofa-bed, my wall desk, my piano, side table/sound station, my workout station/coffee table, and my filing cabinet. I just noticed most of those items have dual functions. More on that later. Now it's time to clean the bedroom.

## BEDROOM

Marie Kondo is a genius. It's so much easier to clean and organize when you can put everything in one place to sort. Since my last clutter-bust, my wardrobe has grown. But not by too much.

I've been very good about keeping a capsule wardrobe, because it works so well for my personality. It's been nine months since I converted, and I've only had one wardrobe freak-out. It was so minor, I hesitate to even mention it. Suffice it to say, my anxiety levels surrounding clothing are basically nonexistent now, and when I think back, I shake my head at all that time I spent freaking out for no reason.

The kids' closet, however… is a monster. Ack. I have to clean this once every six months, since they're growing like weeds, and I usually do it when they're not home if I really want to be efficient, but this time my kids are playing in the room *while I work*. This should be interesting.

Several months ago, my daughter started having anxiety getting dressed in the morning. I could see history repeating itself, and I was determined to make it stop, so I suggested we put her outfits together to make it easier for her to choose… and also to prevent staring from other parents when she goes to school dressed like Ace Ventura.

But I didn't want to cramp her style too much, so I made sure she was part of the process. First, we put all her shirts on hangers, then her pants and skirts. Then, together, we would match them. Once we made an outfit, we'd drape a pair of underwear around the top of the hangers so we could identify the outfit as complete. Then we did this for my son's clothes.

GENIUS!!!

This tool has been so effective, it has cut our morning-routine time in half. We can literally wake up thirty minutes before she needs to be at the bus stop because she no longer hums and haws over what to wear. My son loves it too.

The problem now is that they have more clothes than hangers, so it's time to weed out. I put my daughter on duty, tossing her all the hangers full of shirts.

"Honey, do me a favor and pick out the ones you don't want anymore because we need to make some room."

*But she likes everything.* Negotiating with six-year-olds is an art. You have to think like a one. This is my specialty.

"Well, if you want to get new clothes, you have to get rid of some that don't fit anymore. Tell you what, if you get rid of half the clothes here, we'll have enough hangers left over that we can go thrifting for new ones! What do you say?"

And thirty seconds later, half the hangers are piled to one side.

"These don't fit." She stares at me. "Can I get some princess dresses?"

Okay, so maybe I bribed her.

A promise of two princess dresses later, I can finally address the top portion of the kids' closet. This is where I keep all my toiletries and linens. Cleaning that out is a breeze, using my one-year rule. Half of this stuff I haven't touched since I moved in, but the rest, like dress clothes, will go in storage downstairs. If I still don't use an item and if it's not a total keepsake, like a few of my grandmother's dresses, then I'll eventually donate it, I tell myself. *Yeah.*

Two hours and four donation bags later, our new bedroom looks beautiful and almost Danish. In the room is one dresser, which contains kids clothes. The twin bed and the double bed are neatly made. Toys are in bins, tucked away underneath the beds or piled into one double-drawer unit next to the twin bed. One closet is home to linens and dress clothes I do wear, and the other closet contains all our wardrobes.

It all fits. And it's not crowded, even though the closets are small.

I feel really accomplished right now!

## BATHROOM

A couple of days go by before I decide to tackle the bathroom. I need a break from all this sorting. It's as though cleaning my apartment is like cleaning out my mindbody. It's cathartic and I need time to recover before I begin again.

My bathroom is fairly small, but it feels even smaller with the storage unit above the toilet. It has been home to all my jars of homemade lotion experiments, makeup, and brushes. It's so bulky and invasive, that even when I clean it out it bothers me on an emotional level. I can't explain it.

So I decide to get rid of it.

*But where will I put all the stuff that goes inside?!*

I find an old box and sort out what I use on a daily basis and what I don't. What I don't use on a daily or monthly basis—*if you know what I mean*—goes inside the box and into my closet on the shelf above my hangers. This includes all medicines, jars of anything "extra" and my little box of hair-cutting shears and razor blades for my safety razor. I even include the first aid kit and all the Band-Aids, which I won't get rid of but will always keep to a minimum—because toddlers.

*But what about all this nail polish you've been keeping around for years?*

I decide to throw it out. I haven't used nail polish in nearly a decade, and most of them have separated by now. (Boy, I'm really changing as a person. I never thought I'd get to the point where I don't keep a stash of nail polish. My ex-father-in-law, a biochemist, assures me they're bad for my health and I'm making the right decision.)

It's an hour later and wow! My bathroom looks so much more open and spacious without all the clutter. The small cabinet above the sink houses all my essentials, similar to ZeeDub's in her book *Zero Waste Home*. But there's the issue of cosmetics. She uses a very minimal amount. I use a *fair* amount—too many to fit easily into the cabinet—so I decide to hang them in a three-tiered organizer on my wall. It was made by my aunt in the 1980s, so the fabric is strange and fun to look at. It could pass as art, so there I go again, multipurposing.

I now have seven giant bags of stuff to donate from this month's challenge. It takes me two trips up and down stairs, and all my upper-body and leg strength to move all the bags into the back of my van. I decide to donate to Value Village in particular, because six bags full of items donated gives you a 30-percent-off card. Which makes me sound *really* cheap. I am, inherently. But I am also willing to pay for things I know I will use long term. For example, I paid $250 for a leather purse that also doubles as a duffle bag for work trips, because I know I'll keep it for the next twenty years. And if you break it down, that's like spending twelve dollars and fifty cents per year. Or one dollar and four cents per month. *I can justify anything.*

But I don't need to buy everything new. I'm perfectly happy buying used. It makes me feel better as a human being. It feels right in my soul to use what little I own and let the rest go. Which brings me to my kitchen.

## KITCHEN

Another week goes by and I'm finally tackling my kitchen. The only problem is, there's not much to tackle. It's such a tiny kitchen to begin with, there's no way I could handle excess of anything. And I've discovered that I don't need to.

I have eight glass cups which look very similar to the

ones they serve whiskey in on the train. I didn't swipe them, I promise on my life. They double as cereal bowls for my kids and wineglasses. There are four coffee mugs, three stemless wineglasses (one broke), and eight plates, four salad plates, and eight bowls, all mismatched china I picked up at the thrift store. It's an oddball collection, but it works. It looks so great together, in fact, that I used them in our booth at this year's wedding convention to promote our flower arrangements for work. I got loads of compliments, and one booth designer even copied us.

I also only have six knives to my name: a butcher knife, a bread knife, three paring knives, and one serrated steak knife. That's all I've needed for the past two years because I've never had more than three guests eating over in the past. That could change, once I transform this apartment into the tiny home of my dreams, but I'm not entirely sure it needs to. The only reason I'd need more knives would be if I was planning on serving steaks, and I'm a terrible cook, so I'd probably just serve something like hand salad—what is this craze, people?!—or something I know I can't mess up, like cereal without milk. (Okay, I'm not that terrible! I will order a nice set of steak knives for guests and learn how to cook roast or something. Happy now?)

I mentioned I haven't used paper towels in years, and that still hasn't changed. I've also been using the same cloth napkins my sister made me for the past four years. They're getting quite worn now, so they're extra absorbent and soft.

When my vintage food processor broke, I held off getting a new one since A) I didn't use it often and B) my new blender seems to be just fine at making purees. I'm down to just a few electric items in the kitchen: my cappuccino machine, a waffle iron—in animal shapes because I need to have fun somewhere—a mixer, my blender, a mini smoothie blender which doubles as a protein shake bottle—who wants to clean a huge blender every time?—and a slow cooker. There's still the dehydrator in my hallway closet, but I'm actively looking for things to dehydrate, besides mango. I overdid it last month.

There's not much else to get rid of, folks.

It's funny. Even though there's not much in my apartment compared to before, it still feels full. Not so much in a clutter sense, but in a "lived-in" sense. I hate sterile environments, which is why the idea of minimalism has scared me for so many years. And I wouldn't consider myself minimalist by any stretch, but this is minimalist for me.

Not sterile. Not uninviting. On purpose.

# CHAPTER ELEVEN:
## UPCYCLING AND MULTIPURPOSING
### APRIL 2, 2017

I had to quit social media last year after my *breakthrough*. I don't miss it either. I like being ignorant and uninformed. Now, if I could just quit the news... So I decided it was time to unsubscribe to some of the news outlets that were causing me a lot of pain. Donald Trump managed to become president (America... I don't even...), and the number of email notifications I was getting was out of hand.

While I was unsubscribing, however, I got to thinking about all the shopping sites I had unsubscribed from in month one. You know, the steeply discounted sites like Groupon and Wayfair. I decided it had been a while, so maybe I should visit one or two. You know, to see what I was missing.

I wanted to buy everything I saw! Obviously, I wasn't going to do that. I just worked so hard to clean out my living space a couple weeks earlier! But as I was scrolling through, I couldn't help but notice how specific the functions were of some of the items they were advertising, like kitchen gadgets and furniture that looked cool but didn't serve any other purpose than their one very minor function and to take up room.

And then I had an epiphany!

Nearly every single piece of furniture in my house served dual functions!

1) My fridge is a drawer fridge, which provides counter space on top.

2) My antique refrigerator serves as storage and a display center for my dishes and cutlery.

3) My hinge-top freezer also doubles as a counter space.

4) The entryway seat station doubles as a sewing station storage.

5) The dresser doubles as office storage and a standing desk.

6) The bottom shelf of my wall-mounted shelving unit doubles as my writing desk.

7) Fake flowers taped to pens, pencils, and markers all kept in one bamboo container, double as a bouquet of flowers.

8) A bamboo Kleenex container flipped upside down doubles as a storage box for office supplies, while also serving as a display for the above-mentioned flower/writing utensil bouquet.

9) The stand-alone wardrobe triples as a place to feature my artwork, attached to hangers, and house my favorite magazines and my vision board, while also acting as a room divider.

10) Hangers are used to hold clothes and cleverly display artwork.

11) The twin bed doubles as a ridiculously comfortable sofa.

12) Pillow covers that I designed to house two pillows at a time, to make bed-making faster, also double as floor pillow chairs for movie time.

13) And the coffee table triples as a desk, storage for

my kids' art supplies, and a dip station/box jump station for my home workouts.

Talk about stacking! Or life hacking—whatever the new term is.

This revelation pleases me so much, I decide I'm going to start a new rule right now. *Any incoming furniture must serve more than two functions if it wants to be part of this tiny home.*

Maybe I shouldn't just limit myself to furniture. Now that I think about it, my capsule wardrobe is so effective because many of the pieces offer more than just one function. The pants I designed for my show in Moscow can be worn as pants, cropped pants, or even a long-sleeve shawl, if you're into conceptual fashion, as I am. A convertible dress I made can be transformed from a dress to a top to a skirt to pants, even!

I'm starting to understand that the key to minimalism—*my* kind of "lived-in" minimalism—is making sure that everything surrounding me serves more than just one function. And you know what's fun about that idea? It makes you see the world differently.

I remember telling myself at the beginning of this project that I wanted to find peace in my life through simplification. By transitioning to zero waste, I would get my shit together, in a sense. And in getting my shit together, I would accept my living situation with a little more grace and feel less guilty about that Texas-sized island floating around, covered in garbage.

The thing I'm coming to understand, however, is that *acceptance* doesn't always fix a situation. I'm a born problem solver. I need a certain level of discord in my life to propel me to new heights, creatively speaking. Most of what we use today—cars, furniture, appliances—wouldn't have been born had people just always accepted their lot in life. They didn't accept their situation, so they came up with a solution. So while accepting this new lifestyle, I can now focus more of my time on finding a solution to the problem I don't accept, which is that we're trashing the world.

So, today, I invented a little game. I think it's pretty life changing. If you're a creative person who's stuck, or if you're just looking to get the ol' brain moving again, this could be a good tool to have in the belt.

I'm calling it the GAP test. It stands for Give it Another Purpose. Or maybe I should call it the MPA test. Multi-Purpose Assignment test. I don't know. What's important is how it works.

## GAP/MPA TEST INSTRUCTIONS

Starting in one room, pick a random item and decide what other functions you can assign to it, no matter how ridiculous. One of my earliest examples was a Tetra Pak juice container. After the kids and I emptied it out, I flipped it upside down, cut holes in the top and sides, and turned it into a planter. Then I got excited and saved three months' worth of tea bags and stapled them to an old sheet of poster board. I filled the inside with dirt and started a window garden in my front room.

Another favorite has been using a loofah—yes, the kind you use in the shower—as a pot scrubber. Who knew! It cleans my pots and pans without damaging them, and it's compostable. They make great bath scrubbers when you dunk them in water and sprinkle baking soda on top. I even use them in my soap making occasionally by cutting them into small pieces and inserting them into my soap mold. This way I have a bar of soap and an exfoliator in one.

## MONTHLY UPDATE:

Well, isn't the Universe clever? Remember in month one how I ordered miswak sticks as a possible toothbrush replacement? Well, they never showed up. I emailed the company a couple of months later and never heard back. Then I discovered the company's website shut down a short time after I placed my order. That seemed sort of suspicious, but I never looked for another company, because I was so happy using my bamboo toothbrushes. It wasn't a burning priority, right?

But when I say I'm going to do something, I do it! And this chapter about multipurposing seemed to fit seamlessly with miswak sticks. They're the ultimate multipurpose mouth cleaner. Seven products in one, said that one guy on YouTube.

I had to find out for myself.

I did some digging around and found a clever company in Toronto called Penwak. They sell miswak sticks in two different flavors, original and mint, and they come with a clever little pen-shaped container, hence the "pen" part of Penwak. This allows you to take your miswak stick anywhere and keep it sanitary. I knew immediately I needed two: one for my car and one for my purse. You just never know when you may need to brush your teeth when there's no sink around.

My sticks arrive a few days later. They are individually wrapped, but I'm told I can order them in bulk. First I need to know whether I like the suckers, so I unwrap one, cut off the outer layer, which is surprisingly soft, and chomp on the bristles a few times. I'm chewing on the flavor labeled "original," which I assume is its natural flavor. It tastes twig-y and dully sour. Quite interesting, actually.

It takes a couple chomps to get used to the flavor and to soften the "bristles," but I can finally clean my teeth and gums.

Hot diggity damn! These are really something. I think the miswak industry is a threat to cigarette companies everywhere. Once all the smokers who claim they can stop anytime *if only they could find an oral fixation replacement* try these, all those disgusting cigarette butts on the sidewalk are going to be replaced with twig stumps—which are compostable and non-polluting, by the way, so win/win. En plus, remember all the health benefits I mentioned I found on the internet? They seem legit. Maybe miswak sticks could save the world.

I won't be using them as my only tooth and mouth cleaner, however, because I do love the feeling of peppermint essential oil in my toothpaste. It just makes my mouth feel extra clean. But I will definitely be adding these to my routine. My teeth and gums are going to get really clean during movie night, that's for sure. Look out, fidget cube. You may have met your zero-waste match.

# CHAPTER TWELVE:
## ZERO-WASTE GIFTING
### MAY 7, 2017

Well, as you may have guessed, last year everyone I know received the gift of handmade soaps. After seeing a beautiful display of soap slivers—thin soaps about half an inch thick—on Etsy, I decided to make several different types of soap, cut them into thin bars, and give people sample packs.

I got a couple of reactions.

Mostly people either asked, *"Do I smell bad? Are you hinting at something?"* or, *"Wow, this is amazing, how did you do that?!"*

I felt proud of my hard work. To this day a few of my friends still have their unused soaps sitting in their bathroom because they look so beautiful, they don't want to use them. Either that, or they discovered there's lard in them and they're secretly a little grossed out. (I accidentally gave some lard bars to my Jewish cousins because I'm severely uninformed about these kinds of things. Being the kind "allergy-conscious" person I am, I listed all the ingredients on the packaging. They pointed it out and looked at each other. There was an awkward silence before we all giggled. Oops.)

I wish I could say that I grew a pair and really stuck to the zero-waste gifting principle last year, though. But I totally chickened out. What can I say? I was in an awkward place in my life.

I did imagine how insane it would be to see empty garbage cans the day after Christmas instead of piles of bags full of torn wrapping paper, if that counts for anything. I also managed to wrap things in a way that made it easy to collect all the paper and gift bags afterward for reuse. My zero-wastiness even rubbed off on the kids' dad. He saved all the packing paper from the shipments he received last year and used that to wrap his gifts.

Awwwwwe.

## EXPERIENCES VS. THINGS

One of the coolest zero-waste gift-giving concepts I learned from perusing ZeeDub's videos last year is the giving of an experience, as opposed to a thing.

Light bulb moment here, folks! Trips to museums, concerts, family game activities… I could do that!

Maybe, if my kids received more experiences, there would be less "stuff" in their room to manage. I just needed to find a balance, somehow. *If I could get a little help enforcing the "one new item in, one old one out" rule, I think this could be a genius plan! No more clutter, forever! And maybe I could take the crown for most playful parent!* So I decided to enlist the help of the Cleaning Fairy for **Stage One of OPERATION: Experience.**

The Cleaning Fairy resembles my grandmother on my father's side. Very loving, but very, very firm. If you don't follow directions, there's a consequence… and she doesn't budge. There's no negotiating, haggling, or drama, and unlike me, she remains completely calm and unshakable in the face of screaming six-year-olds. Unless you stick a piece from her favorite board game up your nostril out of curiosity. Then she kinda loses it.

The only problem with Cleaning Fairy is that the person who made up her existence isn't the best at enforcing consequences.

Here's how she's supposed to work: after reminding my kids a second time (eye roll) that they need to clean their room, I gently remind them (clearly living in a fantasy land, here) that if they do not, the Cleaning Fairy will gladly pay them a visit while they're sleeping and pack up all the toys that are left out. She will then give them away to other little children who don't have toys.

This worked for like a week. The kids would scurry around the house and shove their toys into their toy box faster than you could say *Cleaning Fairy*. But then my youngest started having trouble with the concept. If there was a fairy… and she was coming into his room while he was sleeping… and taking away his toys… then that meant she must be a monster, and monsters are scary. So bedtimes became a pain in my ass for a time. No, sweetie. The Cleaning Fairy will not hurt you. She's only here to take away the toys you don't put away. Don't you feel safe now?

*Sick. Just sick.*

Then I started relying on the threats of Cleaning Fairy showing up *without actually picking up the kids toys* at night. My oldest noticed this right away and took full advantage. Being the smarty pants she is, she also noticed that, strangely, the Cleaning Fairy and I both had the same threshold for toy tolerance. We could stand a mess for a really long time, but once the line was crossed, we would purge exactly the same way, just start boxing stuff up and donating it as quickly as possible without taking into consideration how those around us may feel because we were so frustrated.

Tunnel vision runs strong in my family.

So, finally, it happened. One day, when I mentioned I was going to call the Cleaning Fairy, my daughter crossed her arms, threw all her weight onto one hip like she was sixteen, and said, "Mom. C'mon. We know the Cleaning Fairy is you."

I froze. *She better not ask about Santa Claus...*

I tried so hard not to smile, but when you realize your kid is a genius, you can't help it sometimes. We both giggled.

"Don't tell your brother," I said. To which she replied by screaming "Arlo! MOM IS THE CLEANING FAIRY!"

## PHASE TWO OF OPERATION: EXPERIENCE

It could be argued that experiences aren't as valuable as toys, to a kid. A ticket to a museum costs the same as a doll but can't be played with repeatedly. And I don't know about you, but I don't remember any of the museums I attended under that age of eight, so what's the point?

*Family time.*

That's the point.

Connection.

Bonding.

Shared laughter.

And hopefully a digital camera to capture it so when they're frustrated teenagers who think we never liked them, we can go back and give them cold hard proof that no, in fact, we did manage to have a good time or two.

Before the separation, I was sort of "lost" in motherhood. I didn't know who I was as a woman anymore. I was overwhelmed at the thought of taking my kids out by myself on an adventure. Fear of the unknown, fear of everything, which seemed strange, because as a married couple, my ex and I took our kids everywhere.

I also worried I had turned into my mother, who very

openly reminds me and my sister, Josie, that she thought we were cute as little babies, but we didn't really become interesting until after the age of six when she could do creative activities with us. Until that point, our dad did most of the playing with us.

Now, I love my mom. I love her honesty, but I did not want to be that kind of mom. I wanted to be a playful mom, which just isn't really in my nature. I'm just like her. It was a learning process, I'll put it that way.

After a brief relationship with a slightly older—by thirteen years—man with two teenage children a year after my separation, I suddenly felt my tiny kids were a nuisance. How dare I! I couldn't wait for them to be older. I didn't want to worry about diapers anymore. I wanted them to be teenagers, too... and oh my god, I realized I needed to do something about the situation urgently.

So I dumped him.

I didn't need my kids to feel that pressure. I needed to get my behind in gear and figure out an experience we could have together that would bring us closer. Even if that meant Paw Patrol might be involved.

So I decided it was time to go to the EXPO in St. Hyacinth and see the farm animals and the fair!

What a trip! This was the very first time I did nearly everything my kids wanted to do. I didn't say no. I painted their faces (Elsa and Spider-Man) and let them go on all the rides they wanted, and we spent an enormous amount of time playing outside and interacting with all the farm animals. They were kind and patient the entire day, even though we were being roasted by the hot sun, and I have to say, I had the time of my life. I took a few pictures but tried not to use my phone. I wanted to lock these memories deep in my mind.

After some ice cream and a late afternoon lunch, we decided to hit the local pool on the way back to our car.

My kids were not great swimmers at the time, so I was hesitant to take them because I figured they'd try to swim away from me in different directions, forcing me to choose a child. But I outlined the rules very clearly and lovingly, just like the mommy critter in all the Mercer Mayer books, and because they were in such a good mood, they listened.

We had the time of our lives.

No amount of new toys could replace that experience.

Since our first Daycation, I've come to understand that little adventures are very valuable. When my kids start getting cranky or aggressive, I figure it probably has to do with them not getting enough quality attention, so we go do an activity together. Most of the time they're free activities: library, the learning room at the Biodome, or just staying home and playing games.

When my kids feel happy and heard, the lines of communication remain open for the most part.

## ZERO-WASTE GIFTING

This year for the kids' birthdays and Christmas, I decided I'd give them something they could play with, like a toy, something handmade—soap with a toy inside—and a learning experience. All the neighbor kids were virtuosos by age four, and here I hadn't even thought of enrolling my kids in fifteen extracurricular activities per week. What kind of a mother was I?! So I enrolled my daughter in ballet, which I took for fourteen years, so if I loved it surely she would. But my son was still a bit too young to enroll in anything.

My daughter thought ballet was fun enough, but the time slot was terrible and kept us from being able to go anywhere on weekends. So when the New Year came around, I decided I would pick both kids up immediately after school on Mondays and try teaching them piano. I took lessons as a kid and hated them, so I figured I'd try to teach them the way I wanted to learn… by ear.

They love Monday lessons! They learn a new song every two lessons—something simple like Frère Jacques—and they are rewarded with a half stick of gum for every lesson they complete. For the most part it's a great success. They're learning a skill set, we're having an experience together, and it's free. For now.

## WRAPPING UP

Because I was down on myself for not having a zero-waste Christmas, I figured I'd make a better attempt for my son's birthday two months later. I decided not to use wrapping paper or gift bags but to instead explore the Japanese art of wrapping with material, called furoshiki. There are days' worth of video tutorials online, so it was just a matter of whittling down which method I wanted to use.

I had so much fun practicing! I wrapped up books, my daughter's dolls, wine bottles, lunch containers… there's nothing you can't wrap with a nice big scarf. But I think my son was a little confused when he eventually unwrapped his gift. Where did the paper and gift bag go?

ZeeDub uses this furoshiki technique with her children. Her son gives a great demonstration on video of how they wrap their lunches for school every day. So, now, I never worry about the kids losing a lunch box. A cotton scarf can wrap a lunch and be used as a napkin too!

This year, my goal is to use the remaining material I have lying around the house to create furoshiki wrapping clothes. Last year, everyone got soap. This year, everyone's getting even better soap, wrapped in a furoshiki cloth they can reuse. And probably a beeswax-covered reusable saran wrap because those have been pretty handy and easy to make. I can commit to that.

# CHAPTER THIRTEEN:
## REPARATIONS

You know that song by Shawn Colvin called "Sunny Came Home"? Well, I have a particular line from the song stuck in my head these days. The line where the girl in her song says "it's time for a few small repairs." That's one thing I never thought to cover until now... repairing things.

I guess because it's in my nature to repair things as it is? Must be from all those years pulling gadgets from the dump and watching my dad fix them.

But I've also learned that making repairs saves you money and makes you feel valuable. How much money did I save learning to solder wires together so I could fix my then-husband's laptop screen years ago? He must have been impressed because he bragged to all his friends about it for months. That made my heart sing.

Sewing my daughter's stuffed animal together because she wore a hole in it from cuddling it so much not only saved us from a meltdown, but put me in touch with my roots. I envisioned my grandmothers and great-aunts repairing their children's toys and clothes in a quiet room near candlelight, softly humming lullabies.

We've been making repairs since the beginning of time.

Perhaps this should have been mentioned earlier in

the book. But I'm not so sure I need to go into great detail here. We all know making repairs to an item keeps it out of our landfills. But this whole journey towards a zero-waste lifestyle has done far more than keep stuff out of landfills.

This journey has helped repair…well, me.

I'm in a very different point in my life now than when I started this project. I will say that the act of reducing the amount of waste coming into and leaving my home has brought me more in-line with my beliefs. I can feel myself inching closer to the woman I've always wanted to be. And I think I might be more confident in some aspects.

This project also really helped me get through a difficult period in my life. Sure, I abandoned it for a period of time, but life happens. When we fall off the horse, we get back on.

What I'm coming to learn from this experience, however, is that there's no such thing as being 100 percent zero waste. Even ZeeDub produces one jar of trash per year. You can really only control what comes into your living space.

*But that's where the change starts. That's where the innovation starts.* If more of us refuse to bring trash into our homes, won't companies selling us their products be forced to deal with the disposal themselves? (This is an entirely separate book, but I promise it'll be an awesome one.) And if more of the population really took climate change seriously—I HATE TO SCARE YOU, BUT IF EARTH IS GOIN' DOWN, SO ARE WE!!—maybe we could reverse this whole mess. Maybe we could repair the damage we've done to Mother Nature and to each other.

The problem is, we're all so disconnected because life distracts us with work, family, friends, and "stuff," so we continue to put it off.

As long as we aren't immediately affected, why worry about it?

My goal is to ~~indirectly~~ ~~shame~~ *inspire* people to try making little changes to their routine. If I can convince *one family* to switch to compostable toothbrushes… well, it won't be enough, I know. But what if I can convince one family and they can convince one family, and on and on?

Simple changes are totally doable. I don't have to remind you that one is greater than zero.

And what if you want to follow in my footsteps and try transitioning to zero waste over a year, plus or minus a few months, like I did? I can't promise you'll enjoy any of the monthly challenges I put myself through, or that you'll have the same results. Some people do not like safety razors or using a loofah to scrub their pots. But I can guarantee you this: Mother Earth will be satisfied with any and all of your honest efforts. Do what you can. If not just for the sheer fun of trying something new so you can tell your friends an awesome story. Share your successes and your failures so we can all learn. This is merely a starting point.

**So now what, Jaren, are you officially zero waste? You've had twelve months to transition, even though they were out of order. Thanks, life.**

Well. I did find a zero-waste solution to almost everything I use in daily life. But there are two things I can't find zero-waste solutions for, no matter how hard I try: perfectly cooked bacon and safe sex (with others than yourself). And those are two things I'm just not sure I can live without. So if that means I have to keep a garbage can around…

I guess I would say I consider myself zero-waste *aware*. I still have a garbage can. It's small and made of tin and pretty much only contains food scraps until I get back into composting. I also have one for recycling, but it's getting smaller and smaller since I try only to buy things in glass or tin. I take out my "trash" once a month.

So I think the idea of changing one habit per month

worked out pretty well. I was able to transition while raising kids, working, and writing this book. That's gotta count for something.

Here's what we covered, and here's where I succeeded or failed:

1) Shopping with my own containers - SUCCESSFUL

2) Composting - SUCCEEDED AND FAILED. I need to do more research.

3) Found some easy zero-waste cosmetic replacements - SUCCESSFUL

4) Switched to a safety razor – SUCCESSFUL

5) Learned to reduce my waste considerably while traveling - SUCCESSFUL

6) Learned how to make my own cleaning products and soaps - SUCCESSFUL

7) Consolidated my wardrobe to a capsule wardrobe - SUCCESSFUL

8) Found zero-waste solutions for periods and diapering - SUCCESSFUL

9) De-cluttered my home and turned it into the tiny home of my dreams - CLOSE ENOUGH

10) Learned keys to multipurpose living and mastered the art of upcycling - SUCCESSFUL

11) Learned to better balance the art of gifting Experiences vs. Things - SUCCESSFUL

12) Learned the importance of repairing things, including myself - SUCCESSFUL

## What would prevent people from trying to become zero waste?

Repairing and reversing the damage we've done to the world is a tall order. I know from my own experience that the thought alone of *where to start* can be crippling. To some, it's easier to give up than to take a first step. In other cases, people are interested but don't have access to zero-waste stores or even recycling facilities, because of their location.

I know I have an easier time than most because I live in a rather eco-conscious city of at least a million people. I have a wide variety of stores and markets at my disposal. Some people just don't.

But don't let that stop you from finding one thing you can change, even if it's buying a bigger-size yogurt container instead of individually packaged portions. And after you find one thing, try to find another.

And another.

And another. But keep it fun. Reward yourself somehow. I reward myself with chocolate-covered anything and sanity since it doesn't take me forever to clean my apartment anymore.

Still not convinced zero waste can be fun or worthwhile? Lucky for everyone I've been saving the best for last.

Cold.
Hard.
Numbers.

This is the last card in my pocket, folks, so everybody take a deep breath and check out the super-fancy graph below. And, yes, that includes laundry *and* dishes.

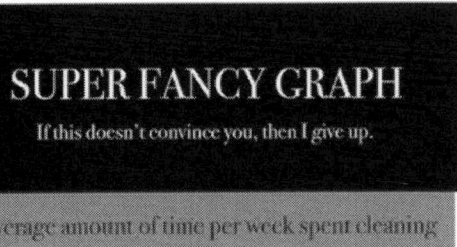

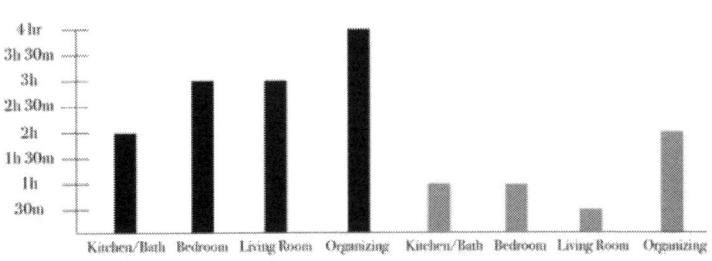

## JANUARY 2016      APRIL 2017

| | |
|---|---|
| 4 hr | |
| 3h 30m | |
| 3h | |
| 2h 30m | |
| 2h | |
| 1h 30m | |
| 1h | |
| 30m | |

Kitchen/Bath   Bedroom   Living Room   Organizing    Kitchen/Bath   Bedroom   Living Room   Organizing

**12h/week**       **4h 30m /week**

# CHAPTER FOURTEEN:
## SIX-MONTH UPDATE

It's hard to imagine it's been six months since I officially finished this transition. I've managed to stick to my zero-waste (90 percent) lifestyle and have even managed to hook my friends along the way.

I've never been pushy with anyone about the subject. I find living an almost zero-waste lifestyle for myself is enough to make me happy, and those who interact with me seem curious enough to absorb it.

One of my dear friends curbed her spending on makeup and instead goes with me to see movies more often.

Another started making her own almond milk.

And yet another decided to switch to a cup after a conversation about zero-waste periods.

These are all small changes I had a part in making, and that makes me feel amazing!

That's change I can see with my own two eyes!

You know how when you buy a car and suddenly start noticing it everywhere? Well, I see zero waste all over these days. Zero-waste chefs, zero-waste entrepreneurs, zero-waste authors.

We're everywhere, you guys. And we're having fun!

So thank you for joining me on this journey. I hope you enjoyed it half as much as I did!

Below, you'll find a list of my favorite zero-waste substitutions, listed by room. To date, I happily use them all.

## KITCHEN

1. Bulk kitchen soap
2. Scrubby made of coconut fibers - OR - loofah
3. Scrubby crocheted from old T-shirts (washable)
4. Hockey towels as a paper towel replace ment
5. Mop with washable mop head
6. Cloth napkins
7. Silicone hot pad which doubles as tooth tab mold
8. Silicone cooking molds (cupcakes, soap molds, baking tray)
9. Beeswax cloth "saran wrap"
10. Reusable drawstring bags
11. Low glasses which double as coffee mug, water glass, bowl
12. Glass jars as containers
13. Tins as containers
14. Refillable wine bottles for bulk wine purchases
15. Spaghetti as disposable coffee stirrers

## BATHROOM

1) Homemade soap
2) African black soap
3) Homemade cosmetics or bulk cosmetics
4) Boar's-hair brush
5) Homemade toothpaste & mouthwash
6) Clay for face mask and hair
7) Loofah
8) Deodorant
9) Cloth pads

10) Diva Cup
11) Homemade skin care (toner and oil)

## ENTRYWAY CLOSET

1) Soap nuts and homemade laundry detergent
2) Homemade soap storage
3) Extra shopping bags (reusable)
4) Thrifted scarves as furoshiki cloths for wrapping gifts

## BEDROOM

1) Capsule wardrobes for me and the kids
2) Clothes made of natural fabrics
3) Thrifted clothing and toys

## LIVING ROOM

1) Multipurposed furniture as listed in Chapter 12
2) Sofa-bed with double pillow covers which convert to floor chairs
3) Window garden (made from tea bags or recyclable bottles)

## CAR

1) Cloth Kleenex
2) Repurposed bin which contains crayons and scrap paper for the kids
3) Kids' potty pot
4) Cloth bags for shopping trips

JAREN CERF

## ABOUT THE AUTHOR

Jaren Cerf is a mother, published songwriter, recording artist, actress, creative director and now author. This is her first book.

She hopes to write many, many more.

JAREN CERF

Made in the USA
Middletown, DE
06 February 2019